100% DEMOCRACY

100% DEMOCRACY

THE CASE FOR
UNIVERSAL VOTING

E.J. DIONNE JR. AND
MILES RAPOPORT

WITH ANALYSIS BY

Cornell William Brooks, Allegra Chapman, Joshua Douglas,
Amber Herrle, Cecily Hines, Janai Nelson, and Brenda Wright

THE
NEW
PRESS

NEW YORK
LONDON

Requests for permission to reproduce selections from this book should be made
through our website: https://thenewpress.com/contact.

Published in the United States by The New Press, New York, 2022
Distributed by Two Rivers Distribution

ISBN 978-1-62097-677-7 (hc)
ISBN 978-1-62097-684-5 (ebook)
CIP data is available

The New Press publishes books that promote and enrich public discussion and
understanding of the issues vital to our democracy and to a more equitable
world. These books are made possible by the enthusiasm of our readers; the
support of a committed group of donors, large and small; the collaboration
of our many partners in the independent media and the not-for-profit sector;
booksellers, who often hand-sell New Press books; librarians; and above all by
our authors.

www.thenewpress.com

Book design and composition by Bookbright Media
This book was set in Sabon and Electra

Printed in the United States of America

10 9 8 7 6 5 4 3 2 1

Contents

Foreword

In the late 1950s and '60s when courts ruled that segregated public facilities, including pools, were unconstitutional, towns and cities often drained their beautiful public pools rather than allow Black children to swim in them, depriving all children of relief from the summer heat and the entire community of a prized public asset.

This theme resonates in so many areas of American life, where laws and practices designed to support racial hierarchies end up hurting everyone, making it impossible, in this wealthiest of countries, for everyone "to have nice things." From the starvation of public education to the subprime mortgage crisis to weak labor unions and low wages, racism has undermined public investment in necessary public goods.

Nowhere has this been more evident than in voting laws and American democracy itself. Contrary to the lofty goals of the nation's founding, the actual design of our democracy has created a system that has depressed the participation and influence of communities of color, and is also far less responsive to the needs of all Americans than the democracy we deserve. Our campaign finance system allows the wealthiest among us—individuals and corporations alike—to have vastly disproportionate influence in our public life. That power imbalance is shown in every sphere of public decision-making, from executive agencies to Congress to state houses across the land.

The great potential counterbalance to the power of money is the power of the people, and particularly the power of the vote. Yet the laws controlling voting have been crafted, in many ways and in many places, to undercut the power of people of color, including hurdles to voter registration, restrictions on voting by mail, and voting prohibitions based on having a felony conviction. And the result of these policies has been an anemic level of voting compared to many other countries, and an electorate that skews heavily toward older, whiter, more educated, and richer voters. The voices of low- and middle-income people, of all races, are far more faintly heard.

Despite all of this, I am hopeful that a very new conversation is beginning in this country—one that, in President Biden's words, "changes the paradigm" that we have been operating under for decades. There is new energy and serious conversation about bold ideas for growing our economy, rebuilding our education system, closing the racial wealth gap, and protecting our planet and our children's future. There is a new moment of possibility for reaping the benefits of what I call The Solidarity Dividend, where we all participate as equals and we all prosper together.

In this wonderful book, E.J. Dionne and Miles Rapoport are proposing to change the paradigm of our democracy in a dramatic and groundbreaking way. They are advocating universal civic duty voting: the idea that every American citizen, as part of her basic civic duties, be required to participate in our nation's democratic life. In doing so, they are calling us to a national conversation about what it means to have truly full inclusion in the decisions that affect our lives. And they make a compelling case that this "100% democracy" will produce the kind of Solidarity Dividends we so desperately need.

I think they are right.

Universal civic duty voting would give us a system in which everyone would count, and the people who represent us would have to speak to *all* of us. The percentages of poor and working people, of young people, and of people from all communities of color participating in voting would jump immediately if universal civic duty voting were adopted, and the voting electorate would look far more like America.

In my opinion, as in the authors', many positive ripple effects would emerge from this one major change. All jurisdictions—federal, state, and local—would have incentives to enact a set of what this book calls "gateway reforms" (such as same day registration and early voting), which would make it more possible and convenient for voters to fulfill their new legal responsibilities.

In addition, I expect a wide range of institutions would respond by promoting participation. Schools would increase their commitment to civic education. Companies would make sure their employees could fulfill their now-required civic duty. Civic and community organizations would make it a larger part of their activities and culture. Media and communications platforms would redouble their efforts to make sure people knew what to do.

The nature of political campaigns would change, too. Now, so much of campaigns are about finding "your" base and getting them to turn out. And, as we have seen all too often, if you can depress the other candidate's or party's base—either by erecting legal or procedural barriers, by negative campaigning, by misinformation, or even by intimidation—well, that's fine, too. But if everyone were voting, guaranteed, campaigns would have to craft messages that appealed to everyone, and voter suppression would become a thing of the past.

And—call me an optimist—I think citizens would respond as well. Young people would develop the voting muscle much earlier, and people would educate themselves, both about procedures and about issues and candidates, in order to be able to fulfill their legal responsibilities. It would become part of the culture, like filling out the census, paying taxes, registering for selective service, and serving on a jury.

Actually, the jury service analogy fascinates me, and seems really important. The reason we have jury duty as a requirement is so that the people who decide on my guilt or innocence, and what penalty is appropriate, will be made up of "my peers." The idea is that we want a fully representative sample of our community to be involved in this most consequential set of judicial decisions. It is part of our culture, we all accept it, and, though people are fond of complaining about being called for jury duty, no one (or almost no one) considers it an unfair infringement on their right not to participate.

The same logic applies, absolutely, to the act of voting. Voters are making decisions just as consequential as the ones made by juries—perhaps even more consequential because of the wide impact of political decisions. We don't, or shouldn't, want a political jury, so to speak, that is heavily weighted toward one segment of our population and which underrepresents key elements of our country's population. It is not surprising, therefore, that the right to serve on a jury—or, more properly, the right *to be compelled* to serve on a jury—was a major goal of the African American community in the civil rights movement. Indeed, that right was fought for in tandem with the fight for the right to vote, won at such great cost.

So does this kind of utopian, "everyone votes," system exist anywhere? Is there a place where all citizens participate all the time, and the voting turnout is 90 percent of eligible voters, rather than the 40–60 percent participation rates that we have come to accept as normal? Well, it turns out that the answer is yes, and in the real world! As the authors examine in detail, twenty-six countries around the globe, in multiple continents, with functioning democracies, actually require participation in elections. And one of them—Australia—has been doing it for one hundred years!

The chapter in this book on Australia is an eye-opening tour. Australia adopted universal voting nationwide in 1924, after several Australian states began to use it in the years before that. Turnouts in Australia have been off the (U.S.) charts, consistently around 90 percent of registered voters, and well over 80 percent of eligible voters, year in and year out. The requirement to vote in Australia has been accompanied by a system that makes registration and voting itself easily accessible. And Australia has succeeded in creating a culture of celebration around elections as full-community affairs. Has universal voting been a panacea for every aspect of democracy in Australia or the other places that use it? Of course not, but it has made just the kind of differences there that the authors predict we would see here. It's hard (but not so hard, really) to believe that a system so successful in a place so much like America has received literally zero attention in the United States. Take the tour in Chapter 4; you'll learn something new, and you'll enjoy it!

I have supported universal civic duty voting for a long time. When I was president of Demos, we began to look seriously at this idea, including its value and its potential challenges in the U.S. and state context. I am proud that we planted the seeds that the Brookings Institution and the Ash Center through the Universal Voting Working Group (which the authors co-chaired) watered and tended so well. Their report, "Lift Every Voice: The Urgency of Universal Civic Duty Voting," broke ground and started the discussion.

With the publication of *100% Democracy*, I believe the flowering of this critical discussion can begin. E.J. Dionne and Miles Rapoport have done all of us a great service by making the case for this game-changing policy as no one has done before. Universal civic duty voting should become a staple of the agenda of organizations trying to improve American democracy, and I hope some truly forward-looking cities and states will embrace and enact the idea, thereby fulfilling their role as laboratories of democracy. I look forward to being a part of this conversation, and I have no doubt that if we can make a democracy that truly reflects the sum of us, we will indeed all prosper together.

—Heather McGhee
author of *The Sum of Us: What Racism Costs Everyone and How We Can Prosper Together*

Introduction

What if We Gave an Election and Everybody Came?

100% Democracy sounds like a grade someone has achieved in a course—and we would like to believe that our American system can be remade to live up to its promise and become worthy of such acclaim.

But the title of this book refers specifically to the aspiration that every American be guaranteed the right to vote—with ease and without obstruction—and that our nation recognize that every citizen, as a matter of civic duty, has an obligation to participate in the shared project of democratic self-government. This book makes the case for what Australians refer to as "compulsory attendance at the polls" and what we call universal civic duty voting.

We see voting as a public responsibility of all citizens, no less important than jury duty. If every American citizen is required to vote as a matter of obligation, the representativeness of our elections would increase. Those responsible for organizing elections would be required to resist all efforts at voter suppression and remove barriers to the ballot box. We believe that universal civic duty voting is the decisive step toward putting an end, once and for all, to legal assaults on voting rights. Civic duty voting would end the cycle of exclusion. It would stop cold the efforts of politicians to invent new legal techniques to keep some of our citizens from casting ballots. And, most importantly, it would engage all American citizens in our democratic experiment. Our call for universal civic duty voting is rooted in the proposition that *rights and duties are intimately related*. To say that everyone *should* vote is the surest guarantee that everyone will be *enabled* to vote. Stressing the obligation to participate will, we believe, expand the freedom to participate. As we will detail in these pages, civic duty voting must be accompanied by other voting reforms. These include expanding same-day and automatic voter registration, early voting, mail-in voting, and no-excuse absentee voting. Such reforms also reduce wait times at polling places, which should be conveniently located and widely available. "Long lines are voter suppression in action," election lawyer Marc Elias observed—one reason the 2014 bipartisan Presidential Commission on Election Administration insisted that no voter should have to wait more than thirty minutes to cast a ballot.[1] We also hope that all states will restore voting rights for citizens with felony convictions.

During Reconstruction and the civil rights era, few reforms were more important or more empowering than ensuring the right of Black Americans to sit on juries. They demanded that they be included in the pool of those who might be *required* to sit through trials because their own liberties depended upon being included in the process of judging whether a fellow citizen would be jailed, fined, or set free. In the case of jury service, the right and the duty are one and the same.

This logic applies to voting as well. The franchise, as one voting rights advocate of the Reconstruction era observed, is "an essential and inseparable part of self-government, and therefore natural and inalienable." W.E.B. Du Bois saw voting as central to the larger aspiration of being treated as an equal, "a co-worker in the kingdom of culture."[2]

Our call to require everyone to vote reflects a sense of alarm and moral urgency in the face of ever more inventive forms of voter suppression. The efforts of Republicans in states they fully controlled to suppress votes by rolling back the reforms that led to the exceptional turnout of 2020 are a national scandal. Their actions demand a forceful response. This book is offered to set our nation down the very different path of full inclusion in our democracy and full participation in its public life. Its proposals are rooted in a spirit of hope—and in a patriotism that takes America's promises seriously.

For it would be a great mistake to see only negative portents in our current situation. As we show in these pages, if some states have tried to push voters away from the ballot box, others have enhanced voting rights by expanding the ways in which citizens can register and cast ballots. These reforms have had a measurable and positive impact on participation—and enjoyed enthusiastic citizen support.

In fact, as our nation showed during the COVID-19 pandemic, when states and localities felt an urgent need to make it possible for their citizens to vote safely and more easily, they could embrace the innovations required to make it so. And when citizens were given more options for casting their ballots, they seized them. In 2020, 159.69 million Americans cast ballots, the largest number in our history. When measured as a percentage of the population eligible to vote, the turnout was 67 percent—the highest in 120 years. We come back to the successes of 2020 in this account as inspiring evidence that Americans will respond in large numbers when given the opportunity to exercise their responsibilities as citizens.

But far from welcoming this achievement and building on it, foes of voting rights looked upon the outpouring of civic energy with horror. Donald Trump's attacks on expanded voting opportunities, particularly by mail, and his false cries of "voter fraud" were part of a mendacious campaign to keep himself in office against the wishes of the majority. His effort culminated in a violent, seditious assault on our nation's Capitol to stop the count of Electoral College votes. Trump's coup attempt failed, and Joe Biden duly took office, but the disgraced ex-president kept his fake fraud campaign going throughout 2021, and it was picked up by many members of his party who had been offering similar arguments to restrict the franchise for more than two decades.

The attacks on the Capitol and the efforts to reverse the wishes of the majority should not be seen as disconnected from American history. On the contrary, Reverend Cornell William Brooks, former president of the NAACP, characterized the mob at the Capitol as voter suppression in action, an attempt to use violence to disempower 81 million voters. The event had deep roots in the tragically successful use of violence in the South after the Civil War to reverse the voting rights revolution of the Reconstruction years and the empowerment of Black Americans.

And while Trump's false charges were repeatedly rejected in court and discredited again and again, attacks on easier access to the ballot began almost immediately after the election in states where Republicans controlled the legislatures. These efforts were especially jarring in Georgia and Arizona, two swing states that Joe Biden won narrowly and where repeated recounts and reviews confirmed what the suppressors refused to acknowledge: that voter expansion had worked and that the vote counts were accurate.[3] The virus of suppression spread to more than a dozen states, including Florida and Texas. Especially pernicious were provisions in some of the bills that allowed partisan majorities in state legislatures to override nonpartisan election administrators and subjected conscientious local officials to fines—simply for doing their jobs. "These new laws are part of a troubling trend to remove authority from election officials who stand up for democracy," University of Kentucky law professor Joshua A. Douglas wrote in the *Washington Post*. "Local election officials know best how to serve their communities. They were the heroes of the 2020 election. It's unfair, inappropriate and unnecessary to punish them with the possibility of fines or jail for protecting the right to vote."[4]

False cries of "voter fraud" never go away, because efforts to disenfranchise parts of the electorate arise again and again. The Capitol mob should not have surprised us, *New York Times* columnist Jamelle Bouie wrote: "As an accusation, 'voter fraud' has been used historically to disparage the participation of Black voters and immigrants—to cast their votes as illegitimate." Those accusations were loud, he notes, after Barack Obama "came to office on the strength of historic turnout among Black Americans and other nonwhite groups. To the conservative grass roots," Bouie added, "Obama's very presence in the White House was, on its face, evidence that fraud had overtaken American elections."[5]

Yes, the fight for inclusion must begin all over again. And universal civic duty voting, we will argue, is the one way to send a message to all Americans that every citizen will count, every vote will be counted, every voice will have a chance to be heard. This is a promise made to economically struggling white voters who may have supported Trump no less than to Black, Hispanic, Asian American, and Native American voters. The United States needs to say, once and for all, that democracy *means* democracy—government of and by *all* of the people.

Many readers no doubt share our belief that high levels of participation are good for a democratic republic and would see as self-evident the assertion that a representative democracy is most representative when everyone participates. But this view is by no means universally held. Some critics fear that near-universal participation would put the nation in the hands of "ignorant voters," a phrase we find both deeply offensive and antithetical to democracy itself. It's no accident that those who tried to bar Black Americans from voting in the Jim Crow era tried to shroud their discriminatory intent behind phony literacy tests and other exclusionary techniques. The "tests" claimed to be about civic competence; in fact they were about denying basic rights.

We see the call to universal participation as rooted in the promises of our founding documents, even if the franchise was sharply limited at the time our republic was born. Recall the Declaration of Independence's insistence on "certain unalienable Rights" secured by governments "deriving their just powers from the consent of the governed."

Our founding republican concept saw government as

legitimate *only* when it was based on the "consent of the governed." Of course, at the Founding, that consent was based on the participation of only white male property owners. But as Martin Luther King Jr. argued, the Declaration amounted to a "promissory note" to *all* Americans.[6] We have spent more than two centuries struggling to make our union "more perfect" and more inclusive.

In this book, we ask what "consent of the governed" means when only about half of the potential electorate typically participates in choosing our leaders—and when even the record-breaking turnout of 2020 still left a third of our potential voters on the sidelines. Since the Voting Rights Act was enacted in 1965 to secure Black citizens' unfettered exercise of the franchise, turnout in the United States has hovered at around 57 percent in presidential elections and 41 percent in midterm elections.[7] In a close election with turnout at 60 percent (the higher end of the norm in most presidential elections), the winner receives votes from only about 30 percent of the population theoretically eligible to vote. In most nonpresidential elections, turnout is typically below 50 percent, meaning that the winning party receives votes from roughly a quarter of eligible voters in a close election and less than 30 percent even in a landslide. Our elected leaders pass laws that affect every aspect of our daily lives. But they derive their powers from a minority of Americans—those who actually cast a ballot. Do those

leaders have true democratic legitimacy, since nonpartici-
pants cannot be assumed to be giving their "consent"?

The sense that our government is less than fully legitimate
creates a vicious cycle: those who doubt its legitimacy might
refrain from participation, but their lack of participation
itself raises questions about the system's legitimacy.

The 2016 American Values Survey, conducted by the Public Religion Research Institute and the Brookings Institution, dramatically illuminated this problem.[8] The survey
asked if respondents agreed or disagreed with the statement
"Politics and elections are controlled by people with money
and by big corporations so it doesn't matter if I vote." The
survey found that 57 percent of respondents agreed with the
statement, including 22 percent who agreed "completely."
Answers to the question were strongly linked to the likelihood of voting. Among likely voters, 48 percent agreed,
and just 15 percent agreed completely. But among those
who were not likely to vote, 72 percent agreed, including
33 percent who agreed completely.

The Knight Foundation's 100 Million Project, an extensive endeavor to understand the attitudes and profiles of
nonvoters, similarly found that nonvoters had lower faith
in electoral systems and lower levels of civic engagement.[9]

Our hope is to replace a vicious cycle with a virtuous cycle
that encourages engagement, creates a more representative
electorate, and tears down barriers to voting. This system

will not instill public confidence in democracy among skeptics overnight. But it is a necessary step, and it has strengthened democratic systems in many other nations.

Boosting turnout, we insist, is not only a matter of justice, representation, and, ultimately, consent. It is also vital to the long-term health of the democratic system itself, a crucial concern at a moment when liberal democracy is under the sharpest challenge it has confronted around the world since the 1930s.

Our nation's struggle to realize the fullness of the franchise began in the battles for the Thirteenth, Fourteenth, and Fifteenth Amendments to the Constitution after the Civil War. They constituted our nation's Second Founding and secured the full rights of citizenship to some of those excluded in our founding documents.[10] The struggle continued with the ratification of the Nineteenth Amendment in 1920, granting women the franchise, and the Voting Rights Act of 1965, prohibiting racial discrimination in voting. Native Americans were not granted full citizenship until the passage of the Snyder Act in 1924 and were not fully granted voting rights until Utah, the last state formally to guarantee the franchise to Indigenous peoples, did so in 1962. Nearly a decade later, when the youngest Americans were being drafted to serve in Vietnam but could not vote, the Twenty-Sixth Amendment extended the franchise to eighteen-year-olds.

The reprehensible police killing of George Floyd in 2020 shocked the conscience of the nation and forced its attention on structural racism. Floyd's death, and those of Rayshard Brooks, Breonna Taylor, and others, called forth large-scale protests around the country against police violence that has long been an enraging fact of life for people of color in the United States. The movement for racial justice is demanding a thoroughgoing overhaul of policing but also a larger confrontation with racism. The call for equal treatment has been reinforced by unequal suffering during a pandemic whose costs to health, life, and economic well-being have been borne disproportionately by communities of color.

Voting rights, equal participation, and an end to exclusion from the tables of power are essential not only for securing reform but also for creating the democratic conditions that would make social change durable. Police brutality, as an expression of systemic racism, is not merely about how Americans are policed but also about whose voices are heard on policing. Universal voting would amplify the long-suppressed voices of voters of color, allowing their perspectives to be represented in the voting booth and enacted in legislatures.

Brooks, the former NAACP president who is now a professor at Harvard's Kennedy School, pointed to an indissoluble link between how our democracy works and how we grapple with every other problem we face. "There is no social justice challenge before the country that is not a democracy challenge," Brooks observed at an event organized for the release of the working group report that forms the basis for this book. "We have seen from Ferguson to Flint that voter rights are at the heart of social justice challenges."

Efforts to exclude Black Americans from the electorate overlap with class inequities. Despite important advances in 2020, Hispanic participation has lagged. And our nation's politics typically place the interests of older Americans, who reliably participate in elections, over the interests of younger generations, who don't. The participation of the young is held down by rules and requirements that are easier for older and more geographically settled Americans to follow and to meet. This, by definition, makes our system less forward-looking. As part of our proposal to declare that all adults are required to vote, we offer many ideas that would welcome Americans under thirty-five into full participation. Since the economic fallout from the COVID-19 pandemic placed particular burdens on young Americans, especially those just entering the workforce, their engagement in the democratic project is more vital than ever.

We begin our account with a look at the lessons of the 2020 election. It demonstrated dramatically both the possibilities of high participation and the threats of voter suppression, the triumph of a free electorate determined to make its voice heard and the unprecedented and ultimately violent effort to set aside the democratic will. The level of turnout showed that expecting every American to vote is realistic—and that the reforms that would accompany this expectation are urgent.

We turn next to the experience of Australia to describe the joys of an Australian election day, and the remarkable achievements of a system that requires citizens to vote. Australia's nearly one hundred years of civic duty voting are proof of concept. The system works, and works well. We move on from Australia to the experiences of other countries and how these might inform an American version.

In the United States, any important innovation is sure to be challenged in court. We thus offer a detailed argument for why we believe universal civic duty voting, properly implemented and enforced, would pass constitutional scrutiny. We make the case that requiring Americans to vote is consistent with our Constitution's guarantees of free speech, robust forms of collective action, and effective government.

We are well aware that the idea of compulsory voting (which, as we will explain later, misdescribes our proposal in important ways) draws a great deal of opposition. A survey conducted in conjunction with the Democracy Fund and UCLA's Nationscape Project makes clear that there is far more opposition than support right now to requiring everyone to vote. At the same time, a large majority of Americans share our view that voting is both a right and a duty. Our conclusion from the data is that while nearly two-thirds of Americans currently oppose mandatory electoral participation, about half the country is at least open to persuasion, a significant opening for a novel concept that has never been advanced in an organized and energetic way.

Since this book is intended to do just that, we use Chapter Seven to offer responses to the legitimate criticisms and practical objections to civic duty voting. We propose, for example, that all who have a conscientious objection to voting would be exempted from the obligation (much as conscientious objectors have been exempted from military drafts) and that all who present any reasonable excuse for not voting would be exempted from any fine. Voters, in our plan, would be free to return a blank or spoiled ballot, and a "none of the above" option would also be included on the ballot itself. Any penalty for not voting without a reasonable excuse would be very modest, and civil rather than criminal.

We go on to outline what we call "gateway" reforms that must accompany a requirement that all Americans vote. Universal civic duty voting should be a spur for a range of changes our system needs. It won't work in an atmosphere of voter suppression.

We then turn to the details of how universal civic duty voting would be implemented, how various levels of government can make it work, and what it will take to get it enacted. We pay particular attention to addressing equity concerns related to penalties. Even a small fine could have a disparate impact on low-income voters, and immigrants' rights activists raise legitimate concerns that noncitizens could find themselves subject to unfair penalties. These concerns shaped our recommendations that the fine for failing to vote be limited to no more than $20; that it could not be compounded over time; and that neither civil nor criminal penalties would be imposed for not paying the fine. Any fine would be set aside for those willing to meet a very modest community service requirement. If the experience in Australia and other nations with versions of compulsory participation can be taken as a guide, very few nonvoters would ever face a fine or penalty. We also detail protections for noncitizens to prevent exploitation of the system by public officials hostile to immigrants. For example, we would protect noncitizen immigrants wrongly listed on the voter rolls from the catch-22 of facing one set of penalties if they voted and another if they didn't.

All this underscores that our emphasis is not on imposing sanctions but on sending a strong message that voting is a legitimate expectation of citizenship. Nations that have embraced carefully implemented versions of universal civic duty voting have enjoyed dramatic increases in participation. "Compulsory voting makes democracy work better," concluded Lisa Hill of the University of Adelaide, "enabling it to function as a social activity engaged in by all affected interests, not just a privileged elite."[11]

"Give us the ballot," Martin Luther King Jr. declared in 1957, "and we will transform the salient misdeeds of bloodthirsty mobs into the calculated good deeds of orderly citizens."[12] As our nation opens its mind and its heart to forms of social reconstruction that were, only recently, far removed from the public agenda, it will, we believe, be open to transformative adjustments to our voting system as well. We stress in our final chapter that we do not pretend universal civic duty voting will solve all the problems facing our democracy. But it would be a major step toward democratic renewal.

The new activism that took root both in response to Trump's presidency and on behalf of civil rights points to the need for a renewed civic life. Universal voting would assist in its rebirth. Citizens, political campaigns, and civil rights and community organizations could move resources now spent on protecting the right to vote and increasing voter turnout to the task of persuading and educating citizens. "What would happen," Kennedy School professor Brooks asked, "if we took the resources now devoted to protecting the right to vote and turning out votes, and instead devoted them to social justice, to movement building? What would our democracy look like?" The question contains its own answer: we would look more like a democracy.

Media consultants would no longer have an incentive to drive down the other side's turnout, which only increases the already powerful forces working to make our campaigns highly negative in character. Candidates would be pushed to appeal beyond their own voter bases—and would not be able to ignore those now labeled as "low-propensity voters." This imperative would raise the political costs of invoking divisive rhetoric and vilifying particular groups. Low turnout both aggravates and is aggravated by the hyperpolarization in our political life that is so widely and routinely denounced. Intense partisans are drawn to the polls, while those who are less ideologically committed and less fervent about specific issues are more likely to stay away.

Democratic politics will always involve clashes of interests and battles between competing, deeply held worldviews. At its best, this is a healthy and welcomed aspect of the democratic project. But by magnifying the importance of persuasion, universal voting could begin to alter the tenor of our campaigns and encourage a politics that places greater stress on dialogue, empathy, and the common good.[13] The overall level of political information would increase as parties and candidates would be required to make their case to those who are currently not part of the electorate. And some citizens, initially empowered by their votes, would be drawn to deepen their participation in other aspects of civic life.

While the polemics around easier voting have often taken

on a partisan cast—and all the more so because of Trump's lies about the 2020 outcome—a number of Republican secretaries of state and many conservatives supported mail ballots and other reforms to ease access to voting during the pandemic. Writing in *National Review* in support of broad participation through no-excuse absentee and drive-through voting during the pandemic, Rachel Kleinfeld, a senior fellow at the Carnegie Endowment, and Joshua Kleinfeld, a Northwestern University law professor, warned: "The United States is already at high levels of polarization and historically low levels of trust in government and fellow citizens. We cannot afford an election our people don't believe in."[14] The Kleinfelds would probably not agree with all we write here, but their intervention captures the spirit behind our proposals.

"We have two possible paths," Joshua Douglas wrote in his book *Vote for Us.* "We can accept that voter suppression is a routine part of our democracy, that entrenched interests will rule the day, and that we, as regular Americans, can't do anything about it." The alternative? "We can recognize that reform *is* possible."[15]

Universal civic duty voting is designed to make reform and inclusion the through line of our political system, clarifying the priorities of election officials at every point in the process. Their primary task is to allow citizens to embrace their duties, not to block their participation. Requiring all citizens to vote would tell our political leaders that their obligations extend to all Americans, not just to those they deem to be "likely voters." It insists that *every* citizen has a role to play in our nation's public life and in constructing our future—that all Americans are included in our Constitution's most resonant phrase, "We the People."

Imagine our society with an election system designed to allow citizens to perform their most basic civic duty with ease. Imagine that all could vote without obstruction or suppression. Imagine Americans who now solemnly accept their responsibilities to sit on juries and to defend our country in a time of war taking their obligations to the work of self-government just as seriously. Imagine a society in which 90 percent or more of our people cast their ballots. They would represent all races and classes and heritages, those with strongly held ideological beliefs and those with more moderate or less settled views. And imagine how all of this could instill confidence in our capacity for common action.

Adopting a system of universal civic duty voting would put all these aspirations within our reach. Now is the time for 100% democracy.

100% DEMOCRACY

Chapter One

What We Learned in 2020
Why Universal Voting Is a Logical and Urgent Next Step

After their experience of voting in Wisconsin's primary in April 2020, at a moment when the COVID-19 pandemic was at full force, voters such as Amina Merchant had no reason to believe that the upcoming presidential election in the fall would be either safe or voter-friendly. Merchant, "wearing a full plastic shield over her face with a paper mask beneath it," as Alison Dirr reported in the *Milwaukee Journal Sentinel*, stood in line for two hours outside Riverside University High School on Milwaukee's east side to vote. It was an important election, because the ballot involved not only the presidential primary but also a bitter contest for a seat on the state's ideologically polarized supreme court.

Merchant, thirty-nine, had every reason to worry about her health, having given birth only two weeks earlier. "I think this is terrible," she told Dirr. "I think it's completely unhealthy. I think everyone's safety is at risk. If you look, nobody is keeping or adhering to the social distancing of six feet, and so I am very worried for everyone's health, including my own."

Waiting in the same line was Jesse Stingl, and he was equally angry. "I felt like they were attempting to suppress me," he said, pointing to the fact that Milwaukee had only five polling stations for the entire city. "I have to weigh whether or not I think my rights are as important as my own safety and the decision to come out here, period," he said.[1]

In many ways, Wisconsin's primary marked the low point of the nation's effort to sort out how to hold an election during a pandemic—but it also provided a lesson that the rest of the country (including, eventually, Wisconsin itself) largely heeded.

In a closely divided state where the two parties had been at sword's point ever since the divisive governorship of Republican Scott Walker, there was disagreement even about whether the election should be held at all. At the heart of the dispute was the state supreme court race, in which conservative incumbent Daniel Kelly, backed by the GOP, faced a vigorous challenge from circuit court judge Jill Karofsky, supported by the Democrats.

Fearing that an election would be hazardous to those who turned out (and concerned about the pandemic's impact on voting in crowded Democratic cities such as Milwaukee), Democratic governor Tony Evers tried at the last minute to suspend in-person voting and postpone the election until June. Republicans, who did not mind at all that the pandemic might diminish turnout in Democratic areas, got that very same supreme court (with Kelly recusing himself) to vote 4–2 to block the governor's order. The vote was along ideological lines. "Justice" and "safety," it seemed, were entirely partisan questions.

In a separate suit regarding the Wisconsin election, the five Republican-appointed conservatives on the U.S. Supreme Court issued an election-eve decision refusing to extend the deadline for absentee ballots. One of the last dissents Justice Ruth Bader Ginsburg would file before her death dripped with sarcasm: "The Court's order requires absentee voters to postmark their ballots by election day, April 7—i.e., tomorrow—even if they did not receive their ballots by that date. That is a novel requirement." In case the conservative justices who wrote the voter-suppression ukase missed her irony, she made quite clear what she was saying: "A voter cannot deliver for postmarking a ballot she has not received."[2]

And lest anyone doubt that this skirmish and others like it were about the fall election, President Trump weighed in on *Fox and Friends* in March 2020 about his fear of what high turnout could mean for him. Explaining why he was resisting the efforts of congressional Democrats to finance nationwide mail-in voting, he warned Republicans about levels of voting such that "if you'd ever agreed to it, you'd never have a Republican elected in this country again."[3] The headline on an account of Trump's comments by the *Washington Post*'s reporter Aaron Blake summed up what the country learned: "Trump just comes out and says it: The GOP is hurt when it's easier to vote."[4] The president—who himself voted by mail in 2018 *and* in the 2020 Florida primary—tweeted that voting by mail, "for whatever reason, doesn't work out well for Republicans."[5]

There was a final prophetic irony in the Wisconsin primary story. Partly because Democrats launched a far more extensive absentee ballot campaign than the Republicans, Karofsky defeated Kelly by a margin of more than 160,000 votes. And in December 2020, the newly elected liberal justice would provide the key votes in 4–3 decisions upholding Biden's Wisconsin victory. During oral arguments on one of Trump's suits—seeking to throw out more than 220,000 ballots in heavily Democratic Dane and Milwaukee Counties—Justice Karofsky admonished Trump's lawyer Jim Troupis: "This lawsuit, Mr. Troupis, smacks of racism."[6] Indeed it did.

Fortunately for the nation's voters, enough election officials in enough states and localities decided that a safe election was in the interest of all their citizens. But Wisconsin's experience, the torrent of litigation by Trump before and after the presidential election to undo the effects of expanded ballot access, and legislative efforts in many states mounted after Biden's victory to reverse pandemic-induced reforms—all point to why we need definitive action to make universal voting a permanent feature of American political life.

The election of 2020—historic, hard-fought, exhilarating, and terrifying all at once—was marked by an exceptional level of controversy and partisan wrangling over the election process itself every step of the way. Figuring out how to conduct a full and fair national election in the midst of the Great Pandemic of 2020 would have been a major challenge in less politically charged times. But there was nothing calm or normal about Trump's presidency and the reactions it inspired. Voters on all sides sensed that the stakes in the election were the highest in memory. For once, the perennial claim about an election being "the most important of our lifetimes" rang true to Americans in large numbers. And because the year also saw a historic racial reckoning after a series of killings of unarmed Black people by police, a "Third Reconstruction" was put on the nation's agenda as well. It was aimed at, finally, fulfilling the promises of the original Reconstruction after the Civil War and the Second Reconstruction that was the civil rights era.

The president began the election cycle by proclaiming that the system was rigged. He ended it by contesting ballots all over the country in dozens of lawsuits. He denounced state and local election officials who refused to fix the election in his favor, and was caught in a recording threatening Georgia's secretary of state with reprisals if additional votes for Trump couldn't be "found." In a denouement that exemplified his lawlessness and disregard for democracy itself, he incited the violent mob that disrupted—but failed to stop—the counting of Electoral College votes. It fell to a surprising Republican dissident, Representative Liz Cheney of Wyoming, to declare that there had never been "a greater betrayal by a President of the United States of his office and his oath to the Constitution."[7] Because she continued to insist on calling Trump's election lies for what they were, she was eventually ousted from the House Republican leadership in May 2021.

In the end, democracy held. People turned out in large numbers. Election officials did their jobs. Courts made decisions in a record number of legal contests that, in the main, supported people's right to vote. All told, more than four hundred lawsuits were filed and adjudicated in forty-four states. Many of them sought to restrict the vote and were strenuously opposed by the voting rights movement. Another large group of lawsuits were filed by voting rights advocates to force open the voting process, allowing and encouraging more people to participate. It was not clear at the outset where the judiciary would land, given the successful effort by Trump and Senate Republican leader Mitch McConnell to stock the courts with conservative jurists. In the end, a substantial majority of lawsuits were decided in favor of opening up the process and making the adaptations necessary to conduct a pandemic election.

Despite the president's frantic rhetoric, the judges hearing the cases and the appeals found virtually no evidence of voter fraud. There was no evidence of any significant interference by foreign actors. Election day itself was calm and chaos-free. And nearly 160 million voters—by far the largest voter turnout ever—made their plans, exercised their expanded options, and made their voices heard. It was a moment of democratic resilience almost across the board. It is clear now that many of the accommodations made to conduct the election in the midst of the pandemic could—and should—become permanent. The election demonstrated that if voters are given more time and more options, they will take advantage of their opportunities. Strikingly, only a minority of ballots were cast on election day—a term that will now have to be replaced with "election season." According to the report "America Goes to the Polls 2020," published by Nonprofit VOTE and the U.S. Elections Project, a remarkable 111 million people—70 percent of voters—cast their ballots either by mail or early-in-person. That compares with 14 percent in 2000 and 40 percent in 2016.[8]

The successful struggles to expand access should be celebrated, but we should also face inconvenient facts. Efforts to enhance participation were contested from the beginning of the pandemic through this moment. Many of Trump's attacks on the election, as Justice Karofsky observed, reeked of racism, as the president sought to throw out ballots cast in cities with large Black populations, including Philadelphia,

Detroit, and Milwaukee. Changes made to accommodate voting during a pandemic were destined to be portrayed by those opposed to them as justified only during a crisis—and, for many, not even then. The Trump Big Lie about the election has had a long and destructive afterlife as one Republican state after another (using a "lack of confidence" in the system among Trump's supporters as an excuse) rolled back not only the emergency changes of 2020 but reforms that began to take hold a decade or more earlier.

The experience of 2020 should thus inspire our nation to take a leap beyond narrow arguments about procedural expansions and restrictions, beyond efforts to turn out one candidate's base and discourage another's, and, most importantly, beyond the fights that have raged since the beginning of the republic over who should have the right to vote. We should make a clear and resounding choice that in the United States of America, beginning now, every citizen should vote. Voting is a fundamental right, not to be abridged—and a fundamental civic duty that every citizen will proudly discharge.

Chapter Two

The Road to 2020
Steps Back, Steps Forward

To understand the voter surge of 2020 and the backlash
it has inspired in many Republican states, it is important
to see it as the continuation of a trend that began at least
a decade earlier. The high turnouts in the midterm election of 2018 and the presidential election of 2020 did not
happen in a vacuum. The reforms easing participation during the pandemic and before were, in part, a response to
efforts to suppress the vote. These can be traced back to the
2010 midterm election in which the Tea Party wave helped
Republicans take control of both houses of Congress and
pick up nineteen more of the nation's ninety-nine legislative
chambers. (Nebraska is unicameral.) In twenty states, the
GOP emerged with a "trifecta": control of both chambers
of the legislature and the governorship. They won full control not only in traditionally red states but also in states
with Democratic or mixed histories—including electorally
pivotal Wisconsin, Michigan, North Carolina, and Pennsylvania. Republicans then leveraged their dominance to write
laws aimed at keeping their party in power at the state level
for as close to indefinitely as they could manage.

The most obvious strategy was aggressive, partisan redrawing of congressional and state legislative district boundaries after the 2010 census. Republican strategists, through a program called Operation REDMAP, had shrewdly focused in the election of 2010 on specific states and specific legislative districts that would allow them to take control of legislatures. The wave carried them to success. This, in turn, would allow them to create the maps for the 2012 elections and the next decade. In Wisconsin, Michigan, Pennsylvania, North Carolina, Florida, and Ohio, gerrymanders gave the GOP lopsided majorities in state legislative and congressional seats, far out of proportion to the party's share of the overall vote. The abuses were especially striking in Pennsylvania and North Carolina, where courts eventually threw out the GOP maps.

But the effort to lock in their power went beyond gerrymandering. A suite of policies was proposed, in varying forms in various states, that had the effect of making it harder to vote. These policies were directed especially against Black and Hispanic voters and young people—traditionally Democratic voters.

The legislative agenda included strict voter ID laws and, in extreme cases, requirements for proof of citizenship in order to vote. The partisan objectives were at times almost comically obvious. In Texas, for example, voters could meet requirements for presenting identification at the polls with concealed-carry gun permits, but not with photo identifications issued by state colleges and universities. Between 2011 and 2020, fifteen states passed laws making voter identification more stringent, with New Hampshire passing one of the strictest voter ID laws, aimed at students, that was struck down by the New Hampshire Supreme Court in 2021. New laws also included limitations on early voting and reductions in the number of polling places. Others added witness and notary requirements for casting an absentee ballot. And then there was the notorious Georgia "exact match" requirement; as the *Washington Post* noted, the law required "that citizens' names on their government-issued IDs must precisely match their names as listed on the voter rolls."[1]

Local and state officials aggressively purged voter lists, a practice that had the greatest impact on people who move frequently or are infrequent voters—the overlapping groups of tenants, low-income people, communities of color, and the young. Voter purges were especially aggressive in Ohio, Georgia, North Carolina, Wisconsin, and Kansas, going well beyond legitimate efforts to remove those who had died or changed residences from the voting rolls.

Kansas secretary of state Kris Kobach became the most visible public figure promoting the falsehood that voter lists were bulging with duplicate registrations, allowing people to vote more than once. He launched an infamous effort called the Interstate Voter Registration Crosscheck

Program, known as "Crosscheck," which encouraged states to purge people whose names were the same as those in other states, with very few safeguards—a program with particular impact on Hispanic and Asian American voters. This effort dovetailed with the strategies of groups such as the American Civil Rights Union (whose name was clearly chosen to be readily confused with the ACLU, the American Civil Liberties Union) that filed suits and pressured election officials to do wholesale purging.

In case after case, however, legal challenges beat back these efforts, notably in Indiana, Florida, and even Georgia.

Indiana is representative. In 2017, the state enacted a law mandating removal of Indiana residents from the voter rolls based on highly incomplete information about a voter's change of address. This voter purge law was based on the unreliable data from Crosscheck. One study estimated that Crosscheck's identification of purported double voters was wrong 99 percent of the time.[2] In June 2018, a federal judge in the Southern District of Indiana issued a preliminary injunction halting implementation of Indiana's voter purge law. And in August 2019, the U.S. Court of Appeals for the Seventh Circuit affirmed the district court's issuance of the injunction, rejecting Indiana's appeal. This ruling meant that Indiana voters were protected from these illegal purges during the 2020 elections. The district court subsequently entered a permanent injunction against Indiana's practices in August 2020.

Eventually, a far better mechanism for interstate checking of voter registrations was created. The Electronic Registration Information Center (ERIC) accomplished the same goals, but with far greater safeguards for voters. By 2020, states were leaving Crosscheck in droves, and as of the fall of 2021, ERIC was implemented in thirty-one states, including Texas.

In the past, the Justice Department had thwarted many of these anti-voter efforts by enforcing key provisions of the Voting Rights Act. But in 2013, five conservative Supreme Court justices, led by Chief Justice John Roberts, gutted the Voting Rights Act in *Shelby County v. Holder*. The decision struck down the act's "preclearance" provision, which allowed the Justice Department to review new voting laws in states and counties with histories of discrimination and voter suppression and to prevent laws or procedures that unfairly restricted the right to vote from going into effect. The *Shelby* decision led to a stampede to enact new vote-limiting laws. The Texas voter ID law, for example, was passed days after *Shelby*.

Research by the Brennan Center for Justice found that between 2014 and 2016, almost 16 million voters were removed from voter registration lists, a 33 percent increase over the number removed between 2006 and 2008. Since *Shelby*, southern states have also closed nearly 1,200 polling places.

Yet the paradox of the past decade is that voter suppression in some states came as other states significantly *expanded* access. And in the absence of an actionable Voting Rights Act, voting rights and democracy groups took on the battle against restrictions themselves, with determination and effectiveness, in the courts and the state legislatures.

A prime example of success was the sound rebuke of the North Carolina legislature, in multiple court decisions, that disallowed its blatantly partisan and racist gerrymanders and struck down other vote-restricting measures as well. In other places, ballot initiatives to reverse or alter some of the worst of the voting policies prevailed in key states. In Michigan, for example, voters passed two initiatives in 2018, one to create a nonpartisan redistricting commission and another to implement a number of voter-expanding policies. In Florida in 2018, voters approved Amendment 4, restoring voting rights to people who had been incarcerated. Activists in Ohio, Kansas, and Georgia battled voter purges even as they spearheaded voter registration drives.

Stacey Abrams became a national figure for her organizing in Georgia. She narrowly lost her race for governor in 2018 in part because Brian Kemp, then secretary of state— who happened to be her Republican opponent—tried to pare back the voter rolls. He left 53,000 voter registration applications "pending," in most cases because of the "exact match" law. It was a move to block new registrants from gaining the right to vote. Lawsuits eventually restored the 53,000 voters to the rolls, but much confusion resulted, and serious damage was done. "The reality is, voter suppression is not simply about being told no," Abrams said at the time. "It's about being told it's going to be hard to cast a ballot."[3] In the end, Abrams lost by 54,723 votes.

After her defeat, Abrams kept on organizing. She persuaded Joe Biden that he could win in Georgia and then played a key role in registering and turning out voters for the Biden-Harris ticket in November. The result was a historic victory in a state that had last voted for a Democratic presidential candidate in 1992. Organizations such as the New Georgia Project, Fair Fight, Pro Georgia, All Voting Is Local–Georgia, Black Voters Matter–Georgia, and many others turned the state into a model of how voter registration and mobilization could transform politics. After the election, Biden declared: "Stacey, if we had ten of you, we could rule the whole world."

He made his comment while campaigning for Democrats Jon Ossoff and Rev. Raphael Warnock in runoff races for two U.S. Senate seats that would determine control of that body. Defying history and much of the punditry, Warnock and Ossoff prevailed. Historically, turnout in Georgia runoffs had been relatively low—and far higher among Republicans than Democrats. The 2021 race upended this pattern to give Democrats their victory.

If organizing was one way to fight voter suppression, legislation was another. In blue states as well as some purple ones, a straightforward agenda to broaden access took shape over the course of the decade. To make registration easier, states expanded opportunities for online registration, established same-day registration, allowed voters to register or to correct or update their registration on election day, set up automatic voter registration systems that greatly facilitated registration at public agencies, and changed the rules to allow sixteen- or seventeen-year-olds to register in advance of an election. Moves to expand the restoration of voting rights for formerly incarcerated people proliferated in many states, most notably in the Florida Amendment 4 success.

Many states also expanded options to cast ballots, providing more opportunities for early in-person voting, including drop boxes for ballots and vote centers that allowed voting for multiple precincts. Even before the pandemic, states were expanding opportunities for voting by mail—for example, by allowing for no-excuse absentee voting, sending ballots to voters in advance of the election, and creating lists of permanent absentee voters, precluding the need for a cumbersome absentee ballot application process for each election.

A chart assembled by the National Conference of State Legislatures illustrates the dramatic policy changes between the years 2000 and 2020. If the number of states requiring

Voter IDs increased by more than two and a half times, from 13 to 34, the number providing for election day registration more than tripled, from 6 to 21, and the number providing for early in-person voting nearly doubled, from 22 to 43. It tells the tale of a nation in struggle between two approaches to voting.

Figure 1: Changing Rules on Ballot Access, 2000–2020

Election Policies	# States, 2000	# States, 2020
Voter ID	13	34
Online Voter Registration	0	40
Election Day Registration	6	21
Early In-Person Voting	22	43
No-Excuse Absentee Voting	22	34
All Mail Voting	1	5

Source: National Conference of State Legislatures

The 2018 Midterm Elections

The 2018 midterm elections saw the highest turnout for midterm contests since 1914—and the 2018 turnout was all the more notable because it was based on a much-expanded potential electorate. The 1914 voter rolls, after all, largely excluded women and Black Americans. Yet even in 2018, the good news about participation was tempered by some not-so-good news.

On the positive side was the startling increase in turnout over the previous midterm elections. According to the U.S. Census, 53.4 percent of eligible voters cast ballots in 2018, compared with 41.9 percent in 2014. (These figures are slightly higher than the generally accepted turnout rates of 50 percent for 2018 and 36.7 percent for 2014, reported by the U.S. Elections Project, but by either measure the leap was enormous.)

A number of factors drove the record turnout in 2018. Reaction to the Trump presidency, which dramatically increased the stakes in politics, was clearly a key force behind the outpouring of ballots. Collectively, Republican candidates for the House of Representatives received roughly 10 million more votes than Republican candidates had received four years earlier, but Democratic candidates received *25 million* more votes than the party's candidates earned in 2014.[4]

As was the case even more dramatically in 2020, easier voting was also a factor. In 2018, 40 percent of voters reported casting a ballot by mail or in person before election day.[5] The states of Oregon, Washington, and Colorado showed how vote-by-mail, same-day registration, and automatic voter registration could all spark turnout.[6]

Some of the largest turnout increases were among groups that typically stay away from the polls in midterm elections.

Table 1: Change in Voter Turnout by Characteristics, 2014 to 2018

Characteristic	2014 Voter Turnout	2018 Voter Turnout	Difference
Total	41.9%	53.4%	11.5%
Age			
18–29	19.9	35.6	15.7
30–44	35.6	48.8	13.2
45–64	49.6	59.5	9.9
65+	59.4	66.1	6.7
Gender			
Male	40.8	51.8	10.9
Female	43.0	55.0	12.0
Race and Hispanic Origin			
White alone, non-Hispanic	45.8	57.5	11.7
Black alone, non-Hispanic	40.6	51.4	10.8
Asian alone, non-Hispanic	26.9	40.2	13.3
Hispanic (any race)	27.0	40.4	13.4
Educational Attainment			
Less than a high school diploma	22.2	27.2	5.0
High school diploma or equivalent	33.9	42.1	8.2
Some college or associate's degree	41.7	54.5	12.8
Bachelor's degree	53.2	65.7	12.5
Advanced degree	62.0	74.0	12.0

Characteristic	2014 Voter Turnout	2018 Voter Turnout	Difference
Citizen Group			
Native-born citizen	42.7	54.2	11.5
Naturalized citizen	34.1	45.7	11.7
Metropolitan Status			
Metropolitan area	41.5	53.7	12.2
Principal city	39.1	52.4	13.3
Balance of metro area	42.9	54.4	11.5
Nonmetropolitan	44.3	52.1	7.7

Source: U.S. Census Bureau, Current Population Survey Voting and Registration Supplements, 2014 and 2018.

As Table 1, drawn from Census Bureau data, shows, the share of eighteen- to twenty-nine-year-olds who voted nearly doubled, from 19.9 percent in 2014 to 35.6 percent in 2018. This brought youth midterm turnout to its highest level in at least three decades.[7] For voters aged thirty to forty-four, the increase was also large: from 35.6 to 48.8 percent.

All racial groups experienced increases, and the largest were, again, among groups with historically low midterm voting rates: Asian Americans and Latinx voters. A study by Univision found that Hispanic turnout nearly doubled between 2014 and 2018 in seven states: Arizona, Colorado, Georgia, New Mexico, North Carolina, Ohio, and Pennsylvania. (All but North Carolina and Ohio would support Biden two years later.) The turnout increases were especially large among Hispanic voters who identified as independents.[8]

But here is where the not-so-good news begins to kick in. Despite their turnout increases, many of these groups continued to be underrepresented in the electorate. The 35.6 percent rate among those under thirty was an achievement in historical terms, but still far lower than the 59.5 percent turnout among voters aged forty-five to sixty-four, and the 66.1 percent rate among voters over sixty-five. Hispanic (40.4 percent) and Asian (40.2 percent) turnout was still well below Black turnout (51.4 percent), which, in turn, was below white non-Hispanic turnout (57.5 percent). To state the obvious: the people who actually vote are still significantly older and whiter than the pool of potential voters.

The electorate also continued to have a strong class skew, with educational attainment a serviceable if imperfect indicator of class position. Table 1 makes clear that the turnout increases between 2014 and 2018 were much lower among voters without high school diplomas—and also among those who graduated from high school but did not attend college—than among college attenders. Even with a 5 percent increase in turnout, only 27.2 percent of Americans with less than a high school diploma voted in 2018. By contrast, those with a bachelor's degree saw their turnout increase by 12.5 percent to 65.7 percent, and those with advanced degrees had a 12 percent turnout increase to 74 percent. In sum, the 2018 electorate tilted even more toward those with educational advantages than did the 2014 electorate.

The Census report should give pause to those who say advocates of universal voting are only trying to hand victory to Democratic candidates. Republicans did especially poorly in 2018 in part because so many of their white working-class supporters failed to cast ballots. By contrast, the 2020 surge of Trump voters, as we'll note in more detail in the next chapter, helped Republicans defeat thirteen incumbent House Democrats who sought reelection. All but one of those had first been elected in the 2018 sweep. In those districts, 2020's higher turnout helped Republicans, not Democrats.

And increased turnout was the story of 2020 overall. The trends that turned 2018 into a landmark for midterm participation would do the same for 2020—in the face of a pandemic.

Chapter Three

The Paradox of a Crisis
How a Pandemic Sparked Election Reform and Record Turnout

The common feeling in April 2020, as we saw in Wisconsin, was that the threat of COVID-19 would inevitably reduce turnout by scaring voters away from the polls. In fact, the opposite proved true because a crisis bred innovation. It sped reforms of the system. It showed what easier access to the ballot could achieve.

The 159.69 million Americans who voted in 2020 reflected a turnout of 67 percent of those eligible to cast ballots, up sharply from the historically impressive (for the United States) 59.1 percent turnout in 2016. Of course, the high turnout of 2020, like the outpouring of 2018, owed a great deal to Donald Trump—in both the antipathy he inspired and the loyalty he galvanized. Joe Biden won some 15.4 million more votes than Hillary Clinton received in 2016. Trump received 11.2 million more votes than he had won four years earlier. While some of these increases were due to a decline in ballots cast for third-party candidates—many of 2016's third-party voters returned to one of the major parties to defeat Trump or to reelect him—the bulk came from new participants.

For some groups, as Table 2 shows, turnout increases between the 2016 and 2020 presidential elections were a continuation of leaps upward in 2018. Generationally, the largest increases were among the young, particularly those under thirty, partly because the young started from a lower base. Older Americans (those forty-five and over) still outvoted younger Americans, but the gap was smaller than in the past. Also striking between 2016 and 2020 was a very large jump in Asian American turnout, and a significant increase in Hispanic turnout. But unlike 2018, the 2020 election saw very significant increases among voters with fewer years of formal education. Voters without bachelor's degrees showed big turnout increases over both 2016 and 2018. As we noted in the previous chapter, this rise in participation among educational groups generally more sympathetic to Trump helped explain the GOP's gains in the House of Representatives even in the face of Trump's defeat.

A number of factors contributed to what were overall historic levels of participation. The urgency of the choice let loose a wave of organizing and spending on both sides. The anti-Trump resistance began organizing from the moment of his election—the vast January 21, 2017, women's marches were the first signs of how extensive the opposition was—and continued throughout his time in office. Theda Skocpol,

Table 2: Change in Voter Turnout
by Characteristics: 2016 to 2020

Characteristic	2016 Voter Turnout	2018 Voter Turnout	2020 Voter Turnout	Difference 2016–2020	Difference 2018–2020
Total	61.4%	53.4%	66.8%	5.4%	13.4%
Age					
18–29	46.1	35.6	54.1	8.0	18.5
30–44	58.7	48.8	64.4	5.7	15.6
45–64	66.6	59.5	71.0	4.4	11.5
65+	70.9	66.1	74.5	3.6	8.4
Gender					
Male	59.3	51.8	65.0	5.7	13.2
Female	63.3	55.0	68.4	5.1	13.4
Race and Hispanic Origin					
White alone, non-Hispanic	65.3	57.5	70.9	5.6	13.4
Black alone, non-Hispanic	59.4	51.4	62.6	3.2	11.2
Asian alone, non-Hispanic	49.0	40.2	59.7	10.7	19.5
Hispanic (any race)	47.6	40.4	53.7	6.1	13.3

Characteristic	2016 Voter Turnout	2018 Voter Turnout	2020 Voter Turnout	Difference 2016–2020	Difference 2018–2020
Educational Attainment					
Less than a high school diploma	35.3	27.2	41.5	6.2	14.3
High school diploma or equivalent	51.5	42.1	55.5	4.0	13.4
Some college or associate's degree	63.3	54.5	69.6	6.3	15.1
Bachelor's degree	74.2	65.7	77.9	3.7	12.2
Advanced degree	80.3	74.0	83.0	2.7	9.0
Citizen Group					
Native-born citizen	62.1	54.2	67.4	5.3	13.2
Naturalized citizen	54.3	45.7	60.8	6.5	15.1

Source: U.S. Census Bureau; Current Population Survey Voting and Registration Supplements: 2016, 2018, and 2020.

the Harvard scholar who had closely studied the rise of the Tea Party, turned her attention to the anti-Trump movement after 2016. She and her colleague Lara Putnam showed how this organizing extended to some of the most Republican areas of the country.[1] In addition, record-shattering amounts of money were spent on the 2020 election. And, importantly for our purposes, governors, secretaries of state, legislatures, and election officials made remarkable adaptations to the pandemic.

As we saw in the previous chapter, there were two Americas when it came to voting going into the 2020 election. One consisted of states that restricted access to the ballot, taking advantage of the *Shelby* decision. In the other America, states made large strides in expanding the possibilities for citizens to register and vote. This contrast set up the 2020 battle that would be waged to the eve of Biden's inauguration—and extended indefinitely by Trump and his followers.

From the earliest days of the COVID-19 pandemic, it was clear that carrying out the 2020 presidential election successfully would require substantial changes in how balloting would take place. If it wasn't safe to go to restaurants or bars, it certainly wouldn't be safe to hold elections in municipal offices, or crowded school cafeterias, gyms, or houses of worship. Major accommodations would be required.

Broadly speaking, the policies needed matched those that the more progressive states had been adopting for a decade: vastly expanding mail-in voting, relaxing the restrictions on "excuses" required for absentee ballots, getting applications or ballots directly into people's homes, and extending the time given to voters to send in the ballots. The new circumstances also required hiring and training additional election workers, since senior citizens, long the stalwarts among poll workers, were most at risk for contracting the virus. All these changes required adequate funding.

In the absence of the voting wars, all these policies might have seemed like common sense—and, to their credit, Republican officials in many states acted that way. But other Republicans, and particularly Trump, saw expanded access as a grave danger.

The battle was joined early on when Congress enacted a vast economic relief and stimulus package in response to COVID-19. An election at a time of a health emergency would be expensive. Running the election properly, the Brennan Center estimated, would take some $4 billion— for equipment, added personnel, printing and postage, and training election officials. Election funding has rarely been a high priority for states and localities, so federal help was imperative.[2] In the first CARES Act, the Congress allocated $400 million to election administration—about 10 percent of the Brennan Center estimate. Election officials hoped that the remainder would be forthcoming. It never came.

As early as March, as we saw earlier, the president began to criticize mail-in voting, and his allies in the states took up the cry. In Pennsylvania, despite repeated pleas from Democratic secretary of state Kathy Boockvar, the Republican legislature declined to make it easier to begin processing mail ballots early. As a result, the reporting of Pennsylvania's tally dragged on for a week after the election. In Michigan, the legislature steadfastly refused to allow an earlier start time for vote counting, relenting at the end of the process, barely—allowing the counting to begin only an extra twenty-four hours earlier.

With Trump claiming in advance that the election would be fraudulent if he lost, the urgency of counting ballots quickly was clear. Michigan's Democratic secretary of state, Jocelyn Benson, proved prophetic in an interview in mid-September. Without mentioning Trump by name, she said: "I am mindful of the fact that every minute that passes between when the polls close and when we do announce those final results provides an opportunity for bad actors to sow seeds of doubt in the electorate about the accuracy of our results and the sanctity of our election."[3] Those seeds blossomed into Trump's ongoing campaign of denial.

Court battles over mail voting were waged all over the country. Republican candidates and parties at the state level, as well as national GOP groups and the Trump campaign, sued in multiple venues to prevent election officials from mailing larger numbers of ballots or even applications, to prevent voters from having additional time to fill out their ballots, and to prevent witness and notary requirements from being relaxed—despite the restrictions against personal contacts because of the virus. In many states, these cases dragged on through multiple appeals, creating widespread confusion over what the procedures for voting would actually be.

One of the most shocking episodes in the mail voting drama came to light in July, when it was disclosed that the newly installed postmaster general, Louis DeJoy, had ordered cost-cutting changes at post offices. These included eliminating overtime, preventing extra trucks from transporting mail after hours, and even dismantling mail-sorting machines at the very moment they would be most needed for the election. It was hard to avoid the conclusion that this was an effort to impede ballots from getting to voters on time and to prevent citizens from sending them in with any confidence that they would be received before election day.

The public uproar from the media, the Democratic Party, and members of Congress was immediate. Pressured at public hearings, DeJoy at first denied there were any problems, and then promised to fix things. In the end, the USPS reported that it delivered 97.9 percent of ballots from voters to election officials within three days and 99.89 percent within seven days. It also claimed that the average time to deliver ballots from election officials to voters was 2.1 days, and from voters to election officials 1.6 days. However, NPR reported that as late as October 29, the USPS was struggling with low on-time delivery rates in urban areas including Detroit and Philadelphia.

Pro-Trump legislators and election officials, for their part, sought to limit the times of early voting and the availability of drop boxes while also closing polling places. They defended the closures in the name of fiscal prudence or public health. Efforts to purge the voter lists continued.

In Florida, the legislature's effort to undo the voters' wishes in restoring the right to vote for previously incarcerated people was especially egregious—and effective. Republicans enacted legislation requiring those who had completed their prison sentence to pay all their outstanding fines, with interest and penalties, before they could register to vote. This effectively negated the impact of the reenfranchisement measure. A majority of those newly allowed to register by passage of Amendment 4 had fines to pay, and the records of outstanding fines were kept in a haphazard and chaotic way. Typically, the authorities could not even tell those eligible for reenfranchisement how much they owed. Litigation over the legislation went all the way to the U.S. Supreme Court, which upheld Florida's vote-suppressing play. In the end, despite a large philanthropic effort to pay off outstanding fines and fees coordinated by the Florida Rights Restoration Coalition, only about 200,000 of 1.4 million eligible citizens had their rights restored. The coalition estimated shortly after the election that only about 50,000 of them actually cast ballots.

The 2020 elections were thus not simply a contest between candidates and political parties, between liberals and conservatives, between competing coalitions and voting blocs. They also entailed a multi-front battle over the most basic and fundamental right: the right to vote itself.

So What Have We Learned?

In American electoral life, highly contested presidential elections have often been followed by a serious, bipartisan review to propose ways of improving the system for the next election. After the 2000 election, a commission chaired by former presidents Jimmy Carter and Gerald Ford led to the Help America Vote Act, passed by Congress in 2002, which provided major funding for new voting machines and other election administration needs. It also created the federal Election Assistance Commission. After the 2012 election, the Presidential Commission on Election Administration, chaired by a bipartisan pair of leading election attorneys, Bob Bauer and Ben Ginsberg, made a series of highly practical recommendations for improvements that would shorten voter waiting times and improve election administration.

The forces for expanding and contracting the electorate will face a showdown in the Biden years as Republican states continue to press for restrictions while other states enact further expansions in registration and voting options. At the federal level, a new Justice Department, even without a new Voting Rights Act, will use the avenues still available to push back against voter suppression efforts, as Demo-cratic-led Justice Departments have in the recent past. After Democrats won their narrow majorities in both houses of Congress, they immediately began pushing for a revised voting rights act, named in honor of John Lewis, and com-prehensive political reforms. The For the People Act passed the House in March 2021 and was later slimmed down in the Senate into the Freedom to Vote Act. Both included pro-visions that closely mirror the gateway reforms we describe later as essential to making Universal Civic Duty voting work. As the year progressed, President Biden was increas-ingly forceful in defending what he called "the sacred right to vote."[4]

A full assessment of 2020, we believe, will tell a story of danger and triumph, of recklessness and responsibility. The attacks on voting access, and the assault on the Capitol and on democracy itself on January 6, 2021, are a signal that the status quo is neither stable nor durable. At the same time, friends of democracy can take heart from how seriously the country takes voting and from the many officials in both parties who, under great stress, chose to act as democratic stewards. In 2021, many of them came under attack for doing so.

The vast majority of election officials—Republican and Democratic alike—worked hard to make the elections safe and secure. In most cases, they made the adaptations necessary to allow people a wider array of possibilities in casting their votes. In the face of pressure from the president himself, Republicans in contested states—most prominently Georgia and Arizona—refused to rig vote counts in Trump's favor by disqualifying legally cast ballots.

Republican and Democratic secretaries of state in Washington, Ohio, Michigan, Pennsylvania, Arizona, and West Virginia allowed expanded voting and undertook the public education needed to let voters know how to "make a plan" and vote. Legislatures in twelve states passed legislation opening up the rules for mail-in voting, and governors in states requiring an excuse to cast an absentee ballot issued emergency declarations making the threat of coronavirus an allowable "health reason" for not voting in person. In total, twenty-eight states changed their voting policies to make it easier for voters to cast their ballots by mail. Many local officials vastly expanded drop box locations, arranged for drive-through and curbside voting, set up mobile voting locations, and more. In one remarkable case, the clerk for Harris County in Texas arranged for a twenty-four-hour drive-through voting center, despite lawsuits seeking to stop him.

If so many election officials were heroic in adapting to the pandemic, their efforts were reinforced by an unprecedented mobilization at the grassroots level to register voters in the face of the virus and get them to the polls. Candidates, both political parties, and a vast array of nonpartisan community groups, civil rights organizations, religious institutions, labor unions, sororities and fraternities, and student organizations—all got engaged. Media outlets and social media platforms bolstered their efforts with major public education campaigns. While the social media platforms have come under legitimate scrutiny and criticism for the deluge of misinformation that passed through their portals, many of them also mounted intensive initiatives to get accurate information to voters about how and when to vote. They published the rules and deadlines and arranged for a flood of text messages, emails, and Facebook reminders.

Corporations and other employers also responded. Many businesses took it upon themselves to let their employees and customers know about how to vote. Initiatives including Just Vote, Time to Vote, and the Civic Alliance gained support from hundreds of corporations. ElectionDay.org earned the support of more than a thousand corporations to allow their employees time to vote or become poll workers. In hospitals, Vot-ER placed hundreds of kiosks in emergency rooms around the country. When the pandemic shut down waiting rooms, doctors wore lanyards asking their patients if they wanted to register.

Just as remarkable, when the federal government and many states failed to provide funding for election administration, a large number of foundations and even individual donors stepped up. They provided direct grants to election administrators to mail applications, bought media time for public service announcements, and even paid for equipment to handle expanded mail-in voting. These are all things that government should have funded directly. But someone had to pay for it all, and these donors did.

Most importantly, the resilience of American citizens was on full display throughout the election period. With fear of the virus as a constant presence, with the rules subject to a welter of litigation and changing by the week, and with the president of the United States issuing claims of voter fraud almost daily, it would have been a reasonable expectation that many would flee the process and just stay home.

They didn't. Instead, they went to work. They volunteered to become poll workers by the hundreds of thousands, from all ages and backgrounds—before the election, on election day itself, and for days and even weeks afterward to count the ballots. Millions of people registered for the first time, even though many of the normal ways of doing so were shut down. And the people voted—in multiple ways and in extraordinary numbers.

Americans care about democracy—deeply and passionately. The forces to expand participation, in the end, proved stronger than those at work to contract it. But those seeking to restrict voting simply picked up where Trump left off. As the Brennan Center for Justice reported at the end of

September 2021, "19 states had enacted 33 laws to make it harder for Americans to vote."[5]

What Donald Trump and his mob could not achieve before President Biden's inauguration threatened to be enacted, piece by piece, through the back door of state-level legislation.

Fortunately, the same Brennan Center report found that the forces for inclusion are also at work: twenty-five states had enacted sixty-two laws that included provisions to expand voting access.

Our nation thus faces a stark choice about voting rights and democracy itself. We embrace the efforts of the democracy and voting rights movements to expand participation and access to the ballot as much as possible. But we also believe that the country has reached a crisis moment requiring an even larger step forward. The persistence of voter suppression makes universal civic duty voting necessary. The hopeful civic energy so visible in 2020 makes this major step toward genuinely full participation possible. Chapter Four tells the story of how another proud democracy has made this approach work for nearly a century.

Chapter Four

Democracy Sausages, Required Voting, and High Turnout
Learning from Australia (Again)

"Voting in Australia is like a party," a voter named Neil Ennis told the *New York Times* in 2018. "There's a BBQ at the local school. Everyone turns up. Everyone votes. There's a sense that: We're all in this together. We're all affected by the decision we make today."

What other country has its electoral process defined by BBQ—even if one voter expressed interest in "more vegetarian options at the sausage sizzles"?[1] "What is voting day without a 'democracy sausage'?" asked Lesley Russell, a longtime Australian political activist and policy specialist, in an email interview. "The sausage sizzle is a way for the local school, hospital, fire brigade, or scout troop to raise funds, and Australians never met an occasion that was not improved with food."

Russell added: "It is possible to vote early and by mail in Australia—but honestly, why would you when voting is a community event? Even if the United States cannot bring itself to consider compulsory voting, the least it could do is turn the first Tuesday in November into a public holiday, and declare it a day for celebrating both the privilege of voting and the local snack food of choice."

Oh yes, and there's culinary variety. "There'll be cakes, there'll be drinks, there'll be pies and pastries and a whole range of comestibles of different types because everybody is there raising money and the atmosphere is actually quite joyful," said Kim Beazley, a former Australian ambassador to the United States and a veteran of Australian politics who once led the Labor Party. "So not only do you get a massive turnout, brought by compulsion, but you also get something of a strange reinforcement of the democratic attitude."[2]

And believe it or not, there is at least some academic evidence that all this partying is good for democracy. One study of a randomized group of American communities found that localities that have voting festivals increase turnout by about 6.5 percentage points in elections where the expected baseline turnout was 50 percent. In low-turnout elections (with expected turnouts of 10 percent), the festivals increased turnout by 2.6 percentage points.[3]

Behind the merriment is an essential democratic lesson. "Compulsory voting is a crucial safeguard to prevent disenfranchisement and discrimination, keeping the government responsive to the broadest representation of citizens," said Claire McMullen, a journalist who is a dual U.S.-Australian citizen, in an email interview. "The U.S. approach of merely encouraging people to vote legitimizes partial participation and, de facto, enables voter suppression. By requiring Australians to vote, the onus is placed on Australia's independent national electoral commission, and the government to a lesser degree, to ensure that voting is accessible and secure for all eligible voters."

Australia's system has drawn many admirers—of various political orientations. Writing in 2020, Ralph Nader, a longtime advocate of civic duty voting, reported he had asked a cab driver in Sydney three decades before: "How do you like living in a country that makes you go to vote?"

"I thought he would complain about overbearing bureaucrats," Nader continued. But that was not the answer he got. "He turned around and gave me an impatient look, replying, 'Why, mate, that's a civic duty.'"

Nader went on to argue that a "great benefit of mandatory voting is that all the ways the politicos and their paymasters scheme to obstruct, repress, delay and inconvenience voting in America . . . become crimes."[4]

At the other end of the political spectrum, the leader of the Canadian Conservative Party, Erin O'Toole, spoke in April 2021 of his interest in Australia's system, without endorsing it outright. "Shouldn't we be following the lead of one of our sort of peer parliamentary democracies, like Australia, and thinking that basic element of citizenship is voting, even if you mark none of the above?" he asked. "I think that's a civic duty that we should encourage. I'm going to look closely at what Australia's been doing."[5]

Yes, Australia's system works. A requirement that everyone has to vote leads not to a dour, eat-your-peas mood
but to a festive celebration of democracy and its capacity to
draw a nation together in saluting self-rule. One of the resonant photos from election day in Australia depicts a group
of voters in the polling booths in bathing suits with surf-
boards at their sides. They do their democratic duty, then
crash back into the waves for another ride.

The United States has learned from Australia before.
The secret ballot is commonly known as the "Australian
ballot." Before secret ballots, voters would come to the
polls with preprinted ballots, usually from political parties or partisan newspapers. The voters' preferences were
known to all—which, not surprisingly, could lead to abuses, including vote-buying on a large scale and opportunities for intimidation. As the Harvard historian Jill Lepore
wrote in a delightful history of American ballots in the
New Yorker:

> Undeniably, party tickets led to massive fraud
> and intimidation. A candidate had to pay party
> leaders a hefty sum to put his name on the ballot
> and to cover the costs of printing tickets, buying
> votes, and hiring thugs called "shoulder-strikers,"
> to tussle with voters. To make sure all that soap
> was paying off, ballots grew bigger, and more
> colorful, so bright-colored that even "vest-

pocket voters"—men who went to the polls with their ballots crammed into their pockets—could barely hide their votes.[6]

There is dispute over exactly who first championed the secret ballot in Australia, as Lepore notes, but the states of Victoria and South Australia adopted it in 1856. It spread to the rest of the country over the next two decades. Resistance to bringing the Australian ballot to America was fierce, coming, one early scholar noted, from "ultra-conservative members of the community, and the machine politicians." The approach to voting we now take for granted was seen, he wrote, as "too complex, cumbersome, and impractical, and surrounds voters with restrictions which practical experiment has shown to be unnecessary." But reformers eventually prevailed, with Massachusetts becoming the first state to adopt it in 1888 (the alternative name for the secret ballot thus becoming the "Massachusetts ballot"). By 1896, Lepore notes, "Americans in thirty-nine out of forty-five states cast secret, government-printed ballots."[7]

Our hope is that universal civil duty voting might follow a similar trajectory. Americans have always been open to good ideas pioneered in other nations. We should be prepared to learn from our Australian friends again.

The history of the idea itself suggests an old truth: every reform is the product of complicated political motivations.

And the origins of the push for the adoption of compulsory attendance at the polls in Australia are contested. The happy and widely accepted version of the story is that civic-minded leaders were concerned when turnout dropped to less than 60 percent in the early 1920s. As a result, Australia adopted a law in 1924 requiring all citizens to present themselves at their polling place on election day and providing for fines at the level of routine traffic tickets for those who did not. Over time, courts and election authorities have established "valid and sufficient" reasons for not voting. They include travel, illness, or religious objection.

But the Australian historian John Hirst poked holes in this anodyne version of history, arguing that the push for compulsion came from the conservative side of Australian politics. Support for it was motivated by alarm that the new and well-organized trade-union-based Labor Party would come to dominate politics. As Hirst wrote:

> The adoption of this system is universally believed to have been a response to shamefully low turn-outs at elections. This is not so. It was first used in Queensland state elections in 1915. At the previous election the turn-out had been a very respectable 75 per cent. It was adopted by a Liberal government [Australia's Liberal party, despite its name, is at the conservative end of the spectrum] because it feared at the next election

the Labor Party for the first time would gain a majority of seats. Labor's great advantage was its large number of campaigner workers who, for no payment, worked to get out the vote; that is, to bring the people to the polls. The Liberals thought to offset this advantage by passing a law to make everyone come. They still lost the election but compulsory voting was law and Labor not surprisingly thought well of it and quickly adopted it as its national policy.[8]

Its adoption nationally in 1924, Hirst argued, again arose from "a fear of what Labor might achieve at the next election." But the Labor Party, seeing advantages for itself, supported the measure, and it "was passed in a rush with almost no debate."[9]

Procedural reforms always have a political effect, and players in the system will always try to game out their impact. In the end, the secret ballot weakened political machines, although they adapted to it and had a much longer life than reformers had hoped. In Australia, conservatives saw advantage to compulsion, but the Labor Party realized that it too had much to gain from a system in which everyone votes. In recent years, Beazley points out, some within Australia's conservative coalition (which brings together the Liberal and National Parties) have urged repeal of compulsory attendance at the polls. But conservative former prime minister John Howard—perhaps informed by Hirst's history, and also by an innate political shrewdness—continued to argue that Labor's close ties with the unions would always give the party an organizational advantage. Compulsory attendance, he insisted, was an approach conservatives should welcome. The system has held.

Conservatives in the United States who have worried about the impact of high turnout on the chances of Republican candidates might pause before rejecting out of hand the reforms proposed here. As we have already seen in the 2020 elections, higher turnout, while helpful to Biden and the Democrats at the presidential level, was beneficial in many parts of the country to the GOP's candidates lower down on the ticket. And to the extent that universal civic duty voting would, on net, increase the share of Black Americans, younger voters, and Hispanic voters, the shift might benefit Republicans in the long run by forcing the party to adapt to demographic changes that are inevitable. Republicans eager to move away from Trumpism might especially welcome this change.

The other bottom line from Hirst's account is instructive too: the ultimate impact of procedural changes on political actors can be unpredictable, which means proposed reforms should be examined on their merits. We believe the merits of broad democratic participation should take precedence in assessing universal civic duty voting.

However one looks at the history of compulsory attendance in Australia, the system clearly accomplished what it set out to achieve. In the 1925 election, the first held under the new law, turnout soared to 91 percent and has hovered around that level ever since. The impact also extended beyond the act of voting. In Australia, citizens are more likely than they were before the law was passed to view voting as a civic obligation.[10] The percentage of ballots intentionally spoiled or left blank is quite low. The Australian experience suggests that when citizens know they are required to vote, they take this obligation seriously. Their sense of civic duty makes them reluctant to cast uninformed ballots and inclines them to learn the basics about issues, parties, and candidates.

Beazley, whose father was a cabinet minister and who was himself first elected to the Australian Parliament in 1980, notes archly in response to criticisms about potentially uninformed voters that being, "in quotation marks, 'informed' about political affairs doesn't actually mean that you are. In fact, a lot of people who consider themselves informed and committed are card-carrying idiots." Beazley also speaks eloquently of how thoughtfully the less politically engaged voters brought to the polls under the Australian system now take their obligations:

I have stood at polling booths for the best part of fifty-five, sixty years now, and from being quite a small boy. And I've never thought for one minute

that the people who file past me and take the cards
I hand to them are disinterested and absurdly
ill-informed. They are engaged. Mentally, they
are engaged. Now, they may have been forced to
become engaged . . . and they don't pay attention
at any other time of the year; they move on with
their private lives and are perfectly happy within
them. But it's not too much of an ask to have you
pay attention for a period of, well, a month.

One of the good things about compulsory
attendance at the polls is that, in our experience, people start to pay attention. So they may
not bring to it the sort of systematic thinking of
somebody who is politically obsessed. But they
do bring to it a sense of their interests and a sense
of the interests of the country.

Beazley added that the success of conservatives in Australian elections should reassure Republicans about the
impact of civic duty voting—conservatives have won seven
of the eleven Australian national contests held since 1990—
but that it would likely push the party toward moderation.
"Their sharp ideology, that would not work," he argued.
"In a situation where there's compulsory attendance at the
polls, the card-carrying QAnon lunacy would go out the
window." Beazley noted of the less politically engaged in

Australia, the United States, or anywhere else that "it's very hard to move them with normal politics; try and move them with lunatic politics."

One of the most careful statistical studies of the impact of Australia's compulsory system was conducted by Anthony Fowler, a professor at the University of Chicago's Harris School of Public Policy. His conclusion:

> Before the introduction of compulsory voting in Australia, election results and public policy were drastically different from the preferences of the citizens. When near-universal turnout was achieved, elections and policy shifted in favor of the working-class citizens who had previously failed to participate. . . . While Australia has largely resolved the problem, inequalities in voter turnout remain in most advanced democracies. Increased turnout has tangible effects on partisan election results and public policies, and those effects will benefit the disadvantaged subset of citizens who otherwise would have abstained from the political process.[11]

The basics of the Australian system are straightforward: it is compulsory for Australians over the age of eighteen to register to vote. In some states, voters are automatically enrolled when they turn eighteen, but registration can also be done online or at any number of government offices (including the post office), and Australia instituted a Federal Direct Enrolment and Update program that assists in registration without individuals needing to complete their own enrollment application. Only voters who are enrolled to vote can be fined for not voting, but resistance to registration is not widespread. According to Australian Electoral Commission figures, in December 2020, 96.6 percent of eligible Australians were enrolled to vote.[12]

Federal elections are held every three years (unless a government calls them early or falls) and always occur on a Saturday. Like many U.S. states, Australia allows early voting and vote-by-mail for those who are unable to cast a ballot on election day.[13] The government also provides mobile voting teams for residents who live in remote areas or are in nursing homes, hospitals, or prisons. In Australia's 2016 elections, about 8 percent of ballots cast were mailed, and 32 percent of votes came from the early-voting period.[14] In the 2019 elections, roughly two-fifths of the votes were cast early. These numbers are similar to pre-pandemic patterns in the United States.[15]

For those casting a ballot on election day, citizens can vote at any polling place in their home state or territory, which they can locate through the election commission's website. Russell adds: "If you are out of state on election day it is also very easy to vote. There are arrangements at voting places—in bigger cities there are specific lines—where you can have your enrollment checked and they have the correct voting papers." When it comes to ensuring that voters are prepared for election day, the commission hosts a website with interactive ballots so that citizens can practice filling one out.[16] Australia has a transferable vote system, meaning that voters number their ballots in order of preference. As a result, being ready in advance is especially useful, although political parties also distribute preference cards as a guide to their supporters.

Unlike the United States, Australia has separate elections for local, state, and federal offices, which, Russell says, makes it easier for voters to concentrate on the specific issues at stake and candidates in the running in particular contests. Like most democracies—but, again, unlike the United States—election administration is nonpartisan.

And Bruce Wolpe, a dual Australian and American citizen who was a Democratic staff member in the U.S. House and served as chief of staff for former Australian prime minister Julia Gillard, points to a key additional benefit of civic duty voting. In the United States, he noted in an email interview, political parties expend substantial sums "to get the vote out—and to get particular voting segments out." In Australia, by contrast, "all the vote is out—and the money has much less of a role in skewing the outcome. Australian elections are therefore structurally cheaper—and structurally cleaner."

When election day comes, voters are generally pleased

with wait times and their experience at the polls—91 percent of those who voted on election day in 2019 reported that they were satisfied with the wait time.[17]

The initial federal penalty for not voting in Australia is A$20 (about US$14). However, an election commission report found that in 2007, only about 13 percent of nonvoters (and thus an extremely small fraction of all eligible voters) ended up paying the fine for abstaining from casting a ballot—the remaining nonvoters all gave valid reasons and were not fined at all.[18] In the Swiss canton of Schaffhausen, where voting is also required, the fine is 6 francs (about US$6). In Singapore, unauthorized abstainers are required to pay S$50 (about US$40) in order to become eligible to vote in subsequent elections or run for office.

Australia's system has not been perfect. By initially excluding Indigenous Australians from the mandate to vote, it had an exclusionary effect. (As with jury duty, discrimination was carried out by *excluding* citizens from compulsion.) Enrollment rates among Indigenous Australians are still lower than for the population as a whole. While nearly 97 percent of all Australian eligible voters are on the rolls, just over three-quarters of Indigenous Australians are.[19] It should also be said that while nonwhite immigration to Australia has increased in recent years, the country is still less racially diverse than the United States. Nonetheless, Australia may well provide the best example of what voting could look like if universal participation were implemented in the United States.

Civic Duty Voting Around the Globe

Australia is far from alone among nations in seeing the system's advantages, and the idea of universal voting is not as distant from the American experience as many might suppose. More than two dozen countries have some form of civic duty voting. Besides Australia, Uruguay and Belgium have civic duty voting policies that led to voter turnout in the 2000s in the 90 percent range. (Voter turnout in most countries is calculated as a percentage of registered voters, but the United States uses the tougher standard of measuring turnout against the entire pool of potentially eligible voters, registered or not. Even taking this difference into account, turnout in the United States is lower than in most other democracies.)

Casting a ballot in countries with civic duty voting is often easier than it is in the United States, as the Australian case suggests. Registering to vote is a straightforward and accessible process, if not always automatic; requesting a ballot or finding your polling place typically does not require calls to your local supervisor of elections or constantly checking online resources to ensure that your polling location has not changed; and voting in person does not mean standing in line for hours.

Countries have adopted civic duty voting for a variety of reasons. Colonial ties often played a role—the Democratic Republic of the Congo, for example, inherited the practice from Belgium. Cyprus adopted this policy for a period of time, influenced by Greece and Turkey. There is also a "neighborhood effect": nations are more likely to adopt compulsory voting if nearby states already do. In Latin America, civic duty voting was first introduced in Central America—in Mexico in 1857, El Salvador in 1883, Costa Rica in 1889, Nicaragua in 1893, and Honduras in 1894; from there it spread southward. As Kathy Gilsinan noted in *The Atlantic*, Brazil, Ecuador, Paraguay, Uruguay, and Peru all enacted compulsory voting laws in the 1930s.[20]

At times, civic duty voting has been adopted as part of a package of broader reforms. Fiji and Thailand established it alongside new constitutions in the 1990s. And it is often implemented for strategic reasons by parties and interests that expect to benefit from larger turnouts. It has been instituted in some cases to bolster the power of the working class, and in others to dilute worker influence.[21]

Universal participation is also part of a distant civic tradition in the United States. In the colonial era, voting was mandatory (for the pool of citizens with the franchise) in Plymouth Colony, as well as in the British colonies of Delaware, Maryland, and Virginia. Following the Declaration of Independence, the first constitution of the state of Georgia included a clause penalizing electoral abstention.[22] Around the turn of the twentieth century, Kansas City introduced a law levying additional taxes on those who abstained from voting, although these were struck down by the Missouri Supreme Court.[23] North Dakota and Massachusetts amended their constitutions to allow civic duty voting legislation; while the practice was never introduced in either state, the amendment allowing for "compulsory voting" is still in the Massachusetts constitution.[24] In 1920, Oregon held a referendum on a constitutional amendment that would have allowed civic duty voting, but it was rejected by voters.[25]

Today, the United States is in the regional minority, as most democracies in the Americas have instituted some form of civic duty voting. These include other large democracies, such as Argentina, Brazil, and Mexico, as well as Costa Rica, Paraguay, and Uruguay. Venezuela and Chile abolished civic duty voting in 1993 and 2012, respectively. In Venezuela, the law went largely unenforced after the 1970s, and the country brought actual practice and the law itself into line by repealing sanctions.[26] In Chile, fines that could run to up to $200 for nonparticipation had led many lower-income voters to avoid registration. In a trade-off in 2012, the requirement was abolished and all eligible voters were added to the rolls automatically.[27] (Our proposal for universal civic duty voting in the United States, which will be detailed in Chapters Eight and Nine, calls for automatic voter registration at the outset, and seeks to avoid Chile's problem by making fines very low and easily waived.)

In Europe, some form of compulsory voting is the rule in Belgium, Bulgaria, Greece, Liechtenstein, Luxembourg, Turkey, and the canton of Schaffhausen, Switzerland. In addition, Italy, Cyprus, Spain, and the Netherlands have all instituted a system of civic duty voting for some period of time.

Table 3: Where Civic Duty Voting Is Used Today

Country or Federal Subunit	Severity of Penalties and Enforcement
Argentina	Low
Australia	Medium
Belgium	Medium
Bolivia	Low
Brazil	Medium
Bulgaria	Stayed by Court
Costa Rica	Low
Dem. Rep. of the Congo	Low
Dominican Republic	Low
Ecuador	Medium
Egypt	Medium
Gabon	Low
Greece	Low
Honduras	Low
Gujarat, India*	Stayed by Court

Country or Federal Subunit	Severity of Penalties and Enforcement
Karnataka, India*	Low
Liechtenstein	Low
Luxembourg	Medium
Mexico	Low
Nauru	High
Panama	Low
Paraguay	Low
Peru	High
Samoa	Scheduled for 2021
Singapore	Medium
Schaffhausen, Switzerland	Medium
Thailand	Medium
Turkey	Low
Uruguay	High

*In Gujarat and Karnataka, the law applies only to select local elections.
Note: This categorization of rule severity is based on data from the Varieties of Democracy project and political scientist and civic duty voting expert Shane Singh's own reading of constitutions, electoral laws, and news sources.

Enforcement and Penalties

Penalties (and their enforcement) vary widely among countries. In some places, the penalty for abstention is a simple fine. Peru, for instance, has three tiers of fines determined by the poverty level of the abstainer's district, ranging from US$6.50 to US$24; those who do not pay their fine can be barred from many public services, including banking and being issued a passport. In Belgium, the first instance of nonvoting can attract a fine of €5 to €10 (about US$5.50 to US$11) and the second €10 to €25, and someone who does not vote four or more times within a fifteen-year period can be disenfranchised for ten years. In other places, nonvoters are barred from obtaining certain public services.

Enforcement of penalties for abstention also varies across countries. In general, countries with steeper penalties for nonvoting are more likely to apply them. Belgium, for example, has not fined or sued nonvoters in nearly two decades. In countries including Costa Rica, Greece, Honduras, and Mexico, voting is required, but there are no penalties for not doing so. In Paraguay, the electoral code says the fine is half of a minimum wage. However, the definition is vague—it appears to mean half of the daily minimum of roughly $11—and is not enforced.

It is common for countries to exempt certain age groups from voting requirements. Those aged seventy and over are not required to vote in Argentina, Bolivia, Brazil, Greece, or Peru. In Ecuador and Schaffhausen, Switzerland, the cutoff age is sixty-five; in the state of Gujarat in India, in Luxembourg, and in Paraguay, it's seventy-five. Argentina, Brazil, and Ecuador further exempt those aged sixteen and seventeen, who are allowed to vote but are not compelled to do so.

In many countries, such as Australia and Belgium, voting is mandatory only for those who are registered, which may not include all residents. In Australia, people without a fixed address, such as seasonal workers or those without permanent housing, are not mandated to register or vote in federal elections. In other countries with civic duty voting, such as Brazil and Peru, it is solely the government's responsibility to maintain accurate and updated electoral rolls. In Belgium, citizens are registered to vote automatically by the government, but foreign nationals who reside in Belgium and wish to participate in certain municipal elections must apply to be added to the electoral register. As a general rule, the mandate to vote is limited to those who are on the electoral rolls.

Finally, countries with civic duty voting usually provide exceptions to the mandate to vote for those with a valid excuse—Australia, as we have seen, is an example. What is considered "valid" varies across nations, but commonly accepted justifications include sickness and disability, natural disasters, travel, and religious belief. The proposal for civic duty voting in the United States laid out in this book recommends the inclusion of a conscientious objector exception as well.

As with all legal requirements, civic duty voting can be tempered with a rule of reason. Shane Singh, one of the leading U.S. experts on compulsory voting, notes in *Beyond Turnout: How Compulsory Voting Shapes Citizens and Political Parties* that "the COVID-19 pandemic led some governments to alter the accepted justifications for not voting." He reports:

> In the Australian state of Queensland, local elections went ahead in March of 2020 during the pandemic. While voting was mandatory per Queensland's compulsory voting law, individuals who were showing symptoms and self-isolating could apply to have the fine waived. Ultimately, Queensland opted not to fine anyone who abstained in the March election alone. For its July 2020 national election, Singapore made special arrangements for elderly people to vote in the morning and those with high fevers to vote later in the day. In late 2020 in Peru, the National Jury of Elections reported that medically vulnerable people, including anyone over 65 years old, would be exempt from the voting requirement in the 2021 general election due to the COVID-19 pandemic. In Bolivia, the maximum age at which compulsory voting applies was lowered from 70 to 60 in the October 2020 national election due to concerns about the susceptibility of elderly people to COVID-19.[28]

Incentive-Based Systems

A few countries, and some American jurisdictions, have attempted to use or considered using incentives, either in conjunction with universal voting or on their own, with decidedly mixed results. Bulgaria experimented with a lottery system in the 2005 parliamentary elections, as did a municipality in Norway in 1995. The Bulgarian lottery offered a variety of prizes including a car valued at €15,000, computer equipment, and mobile phones. Norway awarded one winner a travel voucher worth roughly $1,600. In Bulgaria, turnout declined by nearly 10 percent from the previous election, but in Norway the lottery was associated with a 10 percent increase in the subsequent election.[29] Both eventually abandoned the lottery system.

In 2015 in the United States, the Southwest Voter Registration Education Project launched Voteria, which would award one voter a $25,000 lottery prize for voting in a historically low-turnout Los Angeles County school board election.[30] All who voted in the election were eligible for the lottery. A subsequent study found that among those who knew about the lottery, about a quarter (disproportionately including Latinx voters and low-income voters) said it made them more likely to vote.[31]

In Arizona, the Voter Reward Act was on the ballot in 2006. It would have established a $1 million prize "to be awarded to a randomly selected person who voted in the primary or the general election." But the measure failed by a two-to-one margin.[32]

Other countries have also experimented with nonmonetary incentives. Colombia, for example, has used an incentive system in which political participation earns voters favorable access to public employment and educational opportunities and reduced fees for government services. Voters have priority over abstainers in the case of a tie in university entrance exams. Other things being equal, voters have priority over abstainers in the awarding of state employment, educational scholarships, rural properties, and housing subsidies. The duration of voters' military conscription is reduced by one to two months. And voters get a 10 percent discount on passport fees and tuition at public universities.[33] While there appear to be certain legal impediments to incentives in the United States, some ideas are worth considering. Jonathan S. Gould and Nicholas Stephanopoulos suggest a voucher for every person who casts a ballot, covering the potential costs of voting the way government covers the costs of jury service.[34] Another approach would involve a refundable tax credit for registering to vote. On balance, however, the evidence shows that systems along Australian lines are far more effective in boosting turnout than incentive systems.

Results of Civic Duty Voting

The success of Australia in boosting turnout through compulsory attendance at the polls is not isolated. The evidence from around the world is clear that civic duty voting increases turnout. In countries with medium and high enforcement, turnout is roughly 85 percent. The impact of modest sanctions is made clear in Figure 2 below and has been documented in a variety of empirical analyses.[35]

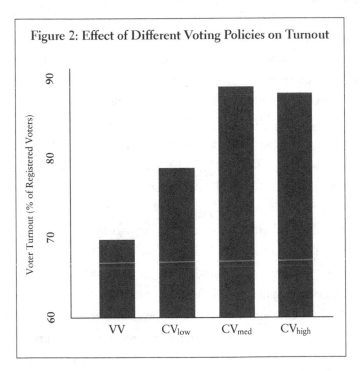

Figure 2: Effect of Different Voting Policies on Turnout

Note: Data and classification of civic duty voting rule severity taken from Version 8 of the Varieties of Democracy Project. VV (Voluntary voting); CVlow (Civic duty voting without sanctions or with sanctions but no enforcement); CVmed (Civic duty voting with enforced sanctions but that impose minimal costs upon abstainers); CVhigh (Civic duty voting with enforced sanctions that impose considerable costs upon abstainers). Included elections are from 1945–2017 in countries considered "Free" by Freedom House.

Civic duty voting also tends to iron out disparities in turn-out along class, ethnic, and racial lines, though this may not be the case when nonmonetary penalties are more likely to affect the upper classes, such as an embargo of passport services.[36]

Unsurprisingly, mandating participation in an election does increase the rate of invalid balloting.[37] In Australia, between 3 and 6 percent of ballots have been declared invalid or spoiled in recent elections, higher than the rate in the United States or Britain—although some of this may owe to the complexities of the Australian transferable vote system.[38] Shane Singh found that the increase in invalid votes is largely "due to the behavior of individuals who are politically unaware and uninterested, individuals who are negatively oriented toward the democratic process, and, especially, individuals who are untrusting of democratic actors and institutions."[39] Spoiled or blank ballots are also often a form of protest, and in the United States, many voters skip voting in down-ballot contests.

Beyond turnout, there is some evidence that where voting is mandatory, voter choices tend to be less reflective of ideological preferences.[40] On balance, it appears that civic duty voting may help the political left, though the studies are divergent, and there is also evidence suggesting that universal voting would strengthen the role of less ideological voters.[41] Mandatory voting is associated with reductions in income inequality, and it has been shown to induce or strengthen psychological attachments to political parties of all stripes.[42] Parties, for their part, are encouraged by the system to place more emphasis on their policies and ideological position.[43]

The bottom line from the evidence: where it has been introduced, universal civic duty voting has largely achieved its purpose of expanding turnout and creating a far more representative electorate.

Claire McMullen, the young US/Australian journalist cited earlier, expressed a mild frustration about explaining Australia's system to Americans and encountering objections from some who viewed "their mystical 'right not to vote' as a form of protest." On the contrary, McMullen argued. Nonparticipation, she said, is "antithetical to a protest in many ways because you are further disempowering and disenfranchising yourself, while arguably giving power to the loudest voices and those with the ability to further marginalize certain groups." She continued:

> I would explain again and again to Americans that in Australia, I can still protest-vote without removing myself from the equation. I can protest by voting for minor parties. I can protest by voting for the party/representatives of my choice. I can protest by voting early or mailing my vote. . . . I can dummy-vote [the Australian term for handing in a blank ballot]. I can protest by not taking

any election flyers when I walk into a voting center. I could protest by not joining the line for a sausage sandwich afterward (but, like not voting, arguably that would only hurt me). But in every "protest" equation, I'm still participating.

McMullen is right: participation in elections is central to self-rule and reinforces the right to protest while making protest more effective. Empowering and enfranchising every citizen is essential to democracy—and civic duty voting, as we argue next, is entirely consistent with our Constitution's design for a free, responsible, and responsive government.

Chapter Five

Establishing Justice, Securing the Blessings of Liberty
Why Civic Duty Voting Is Constitutional

The most underappreciated words in our Constitution are in the Preamble. They define exactly why the founders of our nation established our government and what they expected it to do. The Preamble is at once succinct, ambitious, and clear: "We the People of the United States, in Order to form a more perfect Union, establish Justice, insure domestic Tranquility, provide for the common defense, promote the general Welfare, and secure the Blessings of Liberty to ourselves and our Posterity, do ordain and establish this Constitution for the United States of America."

The first three words, "We the People," are central to the arguments for universal civic duty voting, and a government built on wide participation in our elections would be far more likely to advance the other purposes the Preamble describes—none more so than the quest for justice, domestic tranquility, and liberty.

But as with all far-reaching reforms, civic duty voting would no doubt encounter opposition from those who see it as violating our traditions, the Constitution itself—or both.

It is almost axiomatic about reform in the United States that if a change is important enough, it will be challenged in court. Already, proposals for universal participation in elections have been met with the argument that they would violate the First Amendment—that requiring electoral participation is a form of "coerced speech."

It's thus important to stress at the outset that the proposal outlined in this book is for *mandatory participation* in elections, not *mandatory voting*—a distinction that is central to the analysis offered in this chapter. Thanks to the work of our legal and scholarly colleagues, what follows can be read as a preliminary brief explaining why civic duty voting can and should survive legal challenges. The proposed reform—implemented with the safeguards we suggest—is consistent with the Constitution's guarantees of free speech, robust forms of collective action, and effective government.

Speech or Conduct?

Americans are already accustomed to "attending" or participating in a number of state-required activities: jury duty, registration for Selective Service, the census, schooling for minors, and paying taxes. None of these compel, or stifle, any individual's First Amendment right to speech. The same goes for the requirement of civic duty voting, so long as there is an option to provide an excuse for not participating or to choose "none of the above" on the ballot. The compulsion here is to participate in the election process, not to vote in a specific way.

Courts have interpreted freedom of speech both as a right to engage in certain activity (for instance, the right to protest peacefully and the right to freedom of assembly) and as a right not to have the government require certain expressive activity (the right *not* to speak).[1] With respect to the second framing—the right *not* to speak—the Supreme Court has historically protected individuals from government compulsion to "utter what is not in [their] mind[s]" and ensured their right to "refrain from speaking."[2] For example, public schools may not compel students to pledge allegiance to the flag, drivers may refuse to purchase state license tags with objectionable mottos, and private companies need not advertise for the government.[3]

At first blush, these instances might seem to spell trouble for civic duty voting, if it is not crafted in the right way. Some would argue that a voting requirement (and even an elections participation requirement) could be seen as government-compelled speech, especially if voters must cast a completed ballot that selects a candidate for office. But the Supreme Court, in the cases addressing the three issues just identified, did not outlaw the practices themselves or rule them unconstitutional. They simply forbade punishment for not engaging in the expressive component of the activity. Many schools still conduct pledges of allegiance (but don't force students to participate), and New Hampshire continues to offer "Live Free or Die" license tags (which drivers may cover up). The Court's rulings, rather than requiring states to discontinue speech-related programs entirely, have prohibited the government from punishing individuals for failing to utter the speech at hand—a pledge of allegiance, a state motto, or a government advertisement. The key is that the government may not compel someone to engage in particular expression.

Governments may still impose rules that implicate speech—or require conduct with a speech element—so long as individuals have the ability to opt out of activity that forces expression. Our proposed program doesn't compel voters to choose a particular candidate, or even to fill out a ballot; it only compels them to engage in an act of participation during the election. Universal civic duty voting would not unconstitutionally regulate expressive conduct, because the act of engagement itself—merely participating in an election without requiring a completed ballot—is not inherently expressive. As the Supreme Court has explained in *Spence v. Washington*, communicative conduct receives First Amendment protection only if the speaker had "an intent to convey a particularized message" and "in the surrounding circumstances the likelihood was great that the message would be understood by those who viewed it."[4]

A program that allows individuals to comply with the participation requirement but nevertheless leave the ballot blank, check "none of the above," or write in a candidate (or even a note of objection to the entire process) would not give a hypothetical outside observer any way of determining what message the individual intended to communicate, or if there was a message at all. Conduct that isn't inherently expressive—such that no particular message can be associated with it or, conversely, *any number of* potential messages could be identified with it—does not receive First Amendment protection. In an article on compulsory voting in the *Southern California Law Review*, Sean Matsler noted that "since no one clear meaning can be ascribed to the 'none of the above' option, it is not communicative under *Spence* and therefore not a valid subject of constitutional protection."[5]

As a counterargument, some may claim that the government's compulsion of election attendance—even merely for purposes of signing in—is itself a First Amendment violation. The argument would be that a requirement to show up, with nothing more, still amounts to a form of protected expression in that it demonstrates support for the democratic process generally and for voting more specifically. That argument, though, likely fails for the same reason that claims against filing and paying taxes, showing up for jury duty, or signing up for Selective Service fail.[6] Such requirements, even if speech-related, are governmental mandates to *do* something, not *say* something.[7] Taxes must be paid, juries must be formed, and young men must still sign up for service.[8]

Universal civic participation also entails a requirement to do something, not say something, because the policy would not in fact require voting for a candidate, but instead mandates merely participating in the election in some way. Much as paying taxes does not necessarily entail expression in favor of the tax system, showing up to an election does not necessarily mean that the person is expressing support for the democratic process. A person who refuses to turn out to vote may be doing so for a number of reasons: they may dislike the candidates, think their vote won't make a difference, or even fundamentally disagree with democracy. But the fact of their nonparticipation does not inherently convey any one of these specific messages. Conversely, the conduct of showing up, by itself, is not expressive in the kind of specific way that would implicate First Amendment concerns.

Even if the program as a whole were viewed as speech-related, such that it combines speech (voting) and nonspeech (election attendance) elements, universal civic participation would likely pass constitutional muster because, using the Supreme Court's formulation in *U.S. v. O'Brien*, there's "a sufficiently important governmental interest in regulating the nonspeech element [such that it] can justify incidental limitations on First Amendment freedoms."[9] Civic duty voting furthers an important or substantial governmental interest (full participation in our democratic elections), the governmental interest is unrelated to the suppression of free expression (anarchists may both express distaste and skip the actual selection of candidates, and they can otherwise speak in any way they wish), and the incidental restriction on alleged First Amendment freedoms is no greater than is essential to the furtherance of that interest (because conscientious objectors may opt out of choosing a candidate—and, under the system we propose, have an opportunity to avoid the voting requirement altogether).[10]

As a note in the December 2007 *Harvard Law Review* observed, "requiring someone to vote for a particular cause or candidate would clearly violate the First Amendment, but requiring someone to vote for the candidate of his or her choosing is viewpoint neutral." Such a requirement is thus subject to a laxer level of scrutiny by the courts.[11] The judiciary should view an elections-attendance requirement to be in furtherance of an "important" state interest—namely, the legitimacy that full participation imparts to our democratic processes—that is also "substantially related" to furthering that interest.

The proposal for universal civic duty voting is even less restrictive, given that it doesn't require anyone to cast a completed ballot; voters are free to check in as having participated (in person or by mail) and walk away without casting a ballot. Turnout rates often surpassing 80 percent in countries with comparable universal voting policies speak to the effectiveness of requiring participation in furthering the government's interest in achieving a more representative democracy.[12]

Government's Ability to Regulate Elections

The Supreme Court in *Burdick v. Takushi* held that "when a state election law provision imposes only 'reasonable, non-discriminatory restrictions' upon the First and Fourteenth Amendment rights of voters, the State's important regulatory interests are generally sufficient to justify the restrictions."[13] Although many scholars have criticized this more lenient standard, given that it can allow states to engage in practices that restrict the right to vote, the law as it currently stands should apply just the same to efforts to include more people in the electorate.[14]

Indeed, in the litigation leading up to the 2020 election, the Supreme Court and federal appeals courts demonstrated extreme deference to states in how they sought to administer their elections, even during a pandemic.[15] That same deference should apply if a state seeks to implement civic duty voting.

Some opponents may say that the requirement to attend an election is not minimal, and may even be severe, thereby requiring the Court to evaluate the government program under strict scrutiny. But the government could make the act of "showing up" easier by permitting individuals to check in through a mailed-in form (including government-paid postage) or by some online means (so long as voting itself is not conducted online until doing so is deemed safe and secure by appropriate bodies). The "burden" of checking in is less than the requirement to obtain the documents necessary for a voter ID, which the Court essentially approved in 2008, in *Crawford v. Marion County Election Board*. In that case, the Court found the burden to procure documents necessary to obtain a photo ID to be minimal, and thus viewed the state's photo ID requirement under a lower level of scrutiny.

While one can disagree with the Court on its finding and ruling, as we do—especially since obtaining an ID can, for some citizens, require several trips to government agencies and tens to hundreds of dollars—what's clear is that universal civic duty voting imposes a far smaller burden. The requirement to "attend" an election entails much less action and no monetary payment (a small penalty is imposed only if an eligible voter fails to check in for the election). It must be stressed that requiring *participation* in elections does not negatively impact what some have asserted is the right *not* to vote. If voting were protected by the First Amendment (currently it is not), the right *not* to vote would be protected as well. As voting rights lawyers Armand Derfner and J. Gerald Hebert point out, the Supreme Court hasn't yet explicitly extended First Amendment protections to the right to vote, but that doesn't mean that it will not or that it should not.[16] Indeed, as they observe, "it seems like an obvious proposition that a citizen registering to vote or casting a ballot is engaging in free speech, a fundamental right entitled to full protection under the First Amendment."[17] Moreover, the Court has regularly described voting as a form of speech, even if it hasn't specifically used the word "speech." As Derfner and Hebert explain:

> Supreme Court case law supports a theory of First Amendment protection for voters. The Court has repeatedly characterized the fundamental right to vote in terms of "voice" and expression. In *Wesberry v. Sand*ers, the Court explained: "[N]o right is more precious in a free country than that of having a voice in the election of those who make the laws." In *Reynolds v. Sims*, the Court held: "[E]ach citizen [must] have an equally effective voice in the election of members of his state legislature." In *Norman v. Reed*, the Court noted that voting gives "opportunities of all voters to express their own political preferences." . . . The list goes on at length.[18]

Voting amounts to speech, which *should be* afforded the full protections of the First Amendment. As Janai Nelson, associate director-counsel of the NAACP Legal Defense and Educational Fund, pointed out in a *Florida Law Review* article, since speech in the form of voting is part of the public discourse, First Amendment protection serves the broader goal of democratic legitimacy.[19] Further, adopting civic duty voting, while recognizing the expression inherent in voting for particular candidates, would most likely protect voters from unfair and discriminatory voter suppression practices. But recognizing the right to vote as expressive under the First Amendment would not call into question the constitutionality of civic duty voting, which requires attendance at the election in some form but not the selection of candidates. Again, the core point: attendance is nonexpressive conduct; voting for candidates is the expressive act that would receive First Amendment protection were the First Amendment construed to cover voting rights.

It's impossible, of course, to predict how the current or some future Supreme Court might rule on this issue. The law changes: in the 1960s, for instance, the Court viewed regulations or restrictions on the right to vote under a stricter standard; now, that protection is much less rigorous. But a civic duty voting program, which requires election attendance rather than voting itself, should survive First Amendment review under either the stricter or more lenient standard. Requiring eligible voters to participate in elections would, in fact, *enhance* individual freedom of expression because it would require governments to facilitate registration for all eligible citizens, eliminate laws that actively suppress voters, and ensure that citizens have nonburdensome paths to exercise their franchise.

Monetary or Other Penalties

Monetary penalties, in amounts similar to parking fines, should also survive constitutional analysis. The government would be within its right to charge a small fine in the event an eligible individual fails to participate in the election. (Such a penalty would apply to the individual's failure to check in for the election, either in person, online, or by mail; it would not apply to a citizen's failure to complete a ballot, as that *would* likely amount to a constitutional violation.) State and federal governments routinely impose fees and/or penalties for failure to report for jury duty, register for Selective Service, or pay one's income taxes. In such instances, the government penalizes conduct (or, more precisely, failure to engage in some government-required conduct), not speech.[20] Nonmonetary alternatives, such as community service, should be available for those who would face financial hardship from even a small fine. Another alternative (which is part of our proposal) would be to permit individuals to indicate, by way of a letter or website, a reason for why they did not participate, as is done in Australia.

Incentivizing the Vote

Policymakers should also consider using positive incentives to encourage civic duty voting. Current federal law, however, creates potential roadblocks for using incentives to promote civic duty voting, at least in federal elections. Two federal statutes principally govern the legality of offering benefits for voting: Section 11(c) of the Voting Rights Act prohibits "pay[ing] or offer[ing] to pay or accept[ing] payment either for registration to vote or for voting" in federal elections, and the act proscribes "mak[ing] or offer[ing] to make an expenditure to any person, either to vote or withhold his vote, or to vote for or against any candidate" as well as "solicit[ing] accept[ing], or receiv[ing] any such expenditure in consideration of his vote or the withholding of his vote." The act applies in any election in which a federal candidate appears on the ballot, including those in which a federal candidate is unopposed and in which a benefactor intends payment to influence only the election of state and local candidates.[21]

These federal statutory provisions are clearly aimed at dissuading candidates and interested parties from bribing individuals to vote for or against a particular candidate or ballot measure. This is the context in which they have been applied to date.[22] These provisions have not yet been applied in the context of assessing the legality of a government-offered, viewpoint-neutral, and nonpartisan program to encourage voting participation as an end in itself, without regard to the voter's choice of candidates or ballot measures. Such a program, we believe, would indeed pass constitutional muster.

A promising case in point is a refundable tax credit for people who register to vote—a clear financial incentive, but also clearly nonpartisan, and the incentive is carefully designed to apply not to voting itself but to registration.

Nonetheless, in the absence of changes to these federal laws, experimentation with incentives for voting would be safest, at the outset, in state or local elections where state law does not prohibit such incentives. State supreme court decisions in Alaska and Mississippi have confirmed the legality of incentives under the laws of those states.[23] The Alaska Supreme Court decision noted that California and Washington have similar statutory provisions, prohibiting compensation for voting for a particular candidate, and therefore arguably leaving open the potential of incentives for simply showing up to participate in the election.[24] Several other states have statutory language similar to that of Alaska and Mississippi, including Minnesota, Nebraska, New Hampshire, New Mexico, Pennsylvania, South Carolina, Washington, West Virginia, and Wyoming.[25]

Legal Issues for State and Local Implementation of Civic Duty Voting

One path forward for civic duty voting is for state or local governments to experiment with the idea for their own elections. Indeed, numerous voter expansions, such as women's suffrage and lowering the voting age to eighteen, began at the local or state levels and eventually expanded nation-wide.[26] More recently, other election reforms, such as the use of ranked-choice voting, began at the local level and have now expanded to Maine, Alaska, and New York City. As Supreme Court justice Louis Brandeis wrote: "It is one of the happy incidents of the federal system that a single coura-geous State may, if its citizens choose, serve as a laboratory; and try novel social and economic experiments without risk to the rest of the country."[27] Localities could serve as foun-tains of experimentation on an even smaller scale.[28]

The question remains, however, as to whether state or local law would allow the implementation of civic duty voting. The answer is relatively easy if a state wishes to adopt the practice for statewide elections: states have the authority to regulate their own elections for state offices so long as the rules do not violate the U.S. Constitution or federal law. As discussed previously, there are good reasons to believe that civic duty voting is consistent with the federal Constitution, and no federal statutes would seem to prohibit it so long as it is crafted appropriately (most specifically, to avoid the federal prohibition on inducements for voting). Thus, if a state wished to implement civic duty voting for state elections, it could simply pass a new state constitutional amendment or state law to that effect. We are unaware of any state constitutional provisions that would forbid civic duty voting. Indeed, as we've noted, the Massachusetts Constitution explicitly gives the state legislature the power to provide for "compulsory voting."[29]

The analysis is more complicated, however, if a locality wishes to adopt civic duty voting for local elections. A local government would have to consider both the state constitution and state statutes to determine if it has the authority to mandate participation in local elections. For each of these legal authorities, the locality would have to consider whether there are any state-level legal prohibitions against civic duty voting, as well as whether the locality enjoys "home rule," or the power to adopt its own rules for its own elections.

Localities enjoy only those powers conferred to them under the state constitution or state statutes. In addition, judicial opinions may put a gloss on a locality's home rule powers either generally or for elections specifically.

Regarding substantive prohibitions, there are likely few impediments to civic duty voting unless a court were to read the state's constitutional language on voting extremely narrowly. For instance, the Ohio Constitution provides that "every citizen of the United States, of the age of eighteen years . . . is entitled to vote at all elections."[30] Might a court construe the language "is entitled" in this phrase to mean "is entitled but is not required"? We believe this reading is weak, but we raise it to highlight the potential arguments that proponents might need to refute. Other state constitutions, however, have broader language that make interpretations along these lines even less plausible.[31] In addition, many state constitutions explicitly disenfranchise persons serving felony sentences or mentally disabled individuals, so any civic duty voting rule would need to exclude those individuals unless the state constitution is amended—amendments that, in the spirit of this book, we would recommend.

Our colleagues' review of state constitutions and state statutes suggests that localities in thirteen states may offer the best possibilities for a civic duty voting provision for local elections, though there may be other states where civic duty voting could be implemented. Those thirteen states include Arkansas, California (in "charter cities"), Illinois, Maryland (except in Baltimore), Missouri (only in Kansas City), New Jersey, New Mexico, Ohio, Oklahoma (for cities with a population over two thousand), Rhode Island, South Dakota, Washington (for "first class" cities), and Wisconsin.[32] Washington, D.C., is also a possibility, though as of now Congress has the authority to veto any D.C.-specific laws. In certain states, such as Arizona, Colorado, and Nevada, the question of local authority for election rules is murkier. And other states, such as Connecticut and Maine, have limitations on localities enacting locality-specific voter qualification rules.[33]

We have offered this detailed analysis to make clear our awareness of legal arguments that might be raised to stop civic duty voting. It suggests that opponents could present viable First Amendment or other legal objections if a universal voting proposal is not carefully drafted. But we believe the best reading of the case law shows that a civic duty voting system focusing on the *conduct* of participating in an election rather than requiring a choice of candidates—while avoiding illegal inducements to vote—should pass judicial review.

Chapter Six

The Need for Persuasion
Why the Public Is Skeptical About Universal Civic Duty Voting

It is not unusual for advocates of a new idea to commission polling designed to show widespread public support for the policy they are proposing. We break with that habit here in the interest of honesty and realism. Since our purpose is to change the trajectory of the public conversation about voting and to push a novel idea into the mainstream discussion, we set out to gauge public opinion knowing, in light of earlier surveys, that we would find more opposition than support for universal civic duty voting. We sought to discover which aspects of the idea were most troublesome to its opponents even as we also inquired into public thinking about voting itself—whether it is seen as a right, a duty, or both.

The Democracy Fund and UCLA's Nationscape Project fielded a series of questions in a survey of 6,304 U.S. adults between January 30 and February 5, 2020, in connection with our working group's efforts. The two main findings of the research were in tension with each other. Respondents were asked: "Thinking about voting, which of the following comes closest to your view, even if none of them is exactly right." They were then given three options. Overall, 61 percent said that "voting is a right and a duty," while 34 percent said it was "a right but not a duty." The remaining 6 percent said it was neither a right nor a duty. Thus, a significant majority of Americans agree with our underlying premise: that voting is *both* a right *and* a duty.

But this did not translate into support for a rough version of a proposal for universal civic duty voting that was put to respondents. They were asked: "From what you know, do you favor or oppose the following proposal: Increasing voter turnout by making registration and voting more convenient while also imposing a $20 fine on those who do not vote in a national election. The fine would be waived for those who provide a reason for not voting, such as illness or a moral objection." Overall, 26 percent favored the proposal (including 12 percent who "strongly" favored it and 14 percent who "somewhat" favored it), while 64 percent opposed it—16 percent "somewhat" and 48 percent "strongly."

These results were similar to findings on attitudes toward mandatory voting from the Pew Research Center and You-Gov. In 2018, for example, Pew asked: "Which statement comes closer to your own views—even if neither is exactly right: 'All citizens should be required to vote in national elections' or 'every citizen should be able to decide for themselves whether or not to vote in national elections.'" Pew found that 21 percent agreed with the voting requirement, while 79 percent agreed that the choice should be left to individuals.

The same survey, however, found strong support for making it easier to vote: 67 percent said that "everything possible should be done to make it easy for every citizen to vote." The statement drew support from 48 percent of Republicans and Republican-leaning independents and 84 percent of Democrats and Democratic-leaning independents. Only 32 percent overall picked the alternative statement, "Citizens should have to prove they want to vote by registering ahead of time."

And, in a foreshadowing of the voting changes that would be made during the pandemic, 71 percent agreed that "any voter should have the option of voting early or absentee." The statement drew majorities from both parties: 57 percent from Republicans and Republican-leaners, 83 percent from Democrats and Democratic-leaners.[1]

Support for easier voting was reinforced by the pandemic. A June 2020 Pew survey, for example, found that 65 percent of Americans supported no-excuse early or absentee voting—that is, being able to vote early without a documented reason. An April 2020 Pew survey found that 70 percent of Americans favored allowing any voter to vote by mail if they chose to, and 69 percent favored automatically registering eligible citizens to vote. Americans are clearly ready for such access-easing reforms, even if a majority is not yet ready to embrace a requirement to participate. (Later chapters discuss gateway reforms to ease voting that would make a universal civic duty voting system work.)

In our survey, striking differences were evident in the pattern of responses to the philosophical question about voting as a civic duty and the question about the specifics of a universal civic duty voting plan. The contrasts are clear in Tables 4 and 5 below. Two of the strongest groups supporting the idea of voting as both a right and a duty were at opposite ends of the ideological spectrum—73 percent of those who called themselves "very liberal" and 72 percent of those who called themselves "very conservative." At 69 percent, Republicans and Democrats were equally likely to see voting as both a right and a duty—and were far more inclined to do so than those who did not ally with one of the traditional parties.

On the other hand, the only ideological groups supporting universal civic duty voting itself were those who called themselves very liberal, 51 percent of whom backed the idea, including 34 percent who favored it strongly. Among conservatives, 74 percent were opposed, including 57 percent who opposed it strongly, while 69 percent of very conservative respondents opposed it, including 56 percent who opposed it strongly. Interestingly, there was very little

Table 4: Voting as a Right, Voting as a Duty

Characteristic	Voting is a right and a duty	Voting is a right but not a duty	Voting is neither a right nor a duty
Total	61%	34%	6%
Gender			
Female	62	32	6
Male	59	36	5
Age			
18–29	49	43	8
30–44	56	37	7
45–64	66	30	5
65+	69	28	4
Race			
White	62	33	5
Black	57	37	6
Hispanic	57	35	8
Other	60	33	6
Party ID			
Democrat	69	27	4
Republican	69	28	3
Independent	47	44	9
Something else	34	51	15

Characteristic	Voting is a right and a duty	Voting is a right but not a duty	Voting is neither a right nor a duty
Ideology			
Very liberal	73	23	4
Liberal	67	30	4
Moderate	62	35	4
Conservative	58	36	6
Very conservative	72	24	4
Not sure	34	48	18

Source: The Democracy Fund + UCLA Nationscape Project Survey (6,304 U.S. adults), January 30 through February 5, 2020.

partisan difference on the question: 33 percent of Democrats supported the civic duty voting proposal, as did 29 percent of Republicans. Partisans were slightly more inclined to support the idea than others, no doubt reflecting a greater commitment to the electoral system itself. (This survey, we should note, was conducted in early 2020, before Donald Trump's extensive efforts to deny his defeat with false claims that voter expansions were synonymous with "voter fraud.")

There were no significant differences between white and Black Americans in their attitudes, although Hispanics (at 34 percent support) were more sympathetic to a voting requirement than other Americans.

The largest disjunction between answers on the two questions was generational. Support for the idea that voting was

Table 5: Attitudes Toward Civic Duty Voting

Characteristic	Strongly favor	Somewhat favor	Somewhat oppose	Strongly oppose	Don't know
Total	12%	14%	16%	48%	10%
Gender					
Female	9	14	18	49	10
Male	16	15	13	46	10
Age					
18–29	13	18	18	37	14
30–44	17	16	15	41	11
45–64	12	12	16	52	9
65+	6	12	14	60	8
Race					
White	11	14	15	52	8
Black	15	13	12	47	13
Hispanic	18	16	14	38	14
Other	7	19	25	33	17
Party ID					
Democrat	15	18	17	42	8
Republican	15	14	16	48	7
Independent	7	11	16	52	14
Something else	5	9	10	56	20

Characteristic	Strongly favor	Somewhat favor	Somewhat oppose	Strongly oppose	Don't know
Idealogy					
Very liberal	34	17	13	29	7
Liberal	13	22	19	40	6
Moderate	10	15	16	50	8
Conservative	9	10	17	57	8
Very conservative	14	10	13	56	7
Not sure	6	7	12	44	31

Source: The Democracy Fund + UCLA Nationscape Project Survey.

both a right and a duty rose steadily with age. At opposite ends were Americans under thirty years old, only 49 percent of whom saw voting as both a right and a duty, and Americans sixty-five and older, 69 percent of whom saw voting as both a right and a duty. This squares with other findings— not only in the United States but also around the democratic world—of an increasing skepticism among younger citizens toward electoral politics.[2]

On the other hand, Americans under thirty were far more open to civic duty voting. Only 37 percent of them were strongly opposed to the proposal, compared with 60 percent of those sixty-five and over. When those "somewhat" opposed are added in, Americans under thirty rejected civic duty voting by a margin of 55 percent to 31 percent, while those over sixty-five opposed it by 74 percent to 18 percent.

The upshot is that younger Americans, perhaps because of their skepticism about the current system, may be more open to proposals for fundamental reform. Older Americans are more inclined to support the system as is and are therefore especially wary of large-scale changes. On the other hand, those over sixty-five are the group most sympathetic to the civic values that underlie civic duty voting. Thus, there are avenues of persuasion at both ends of the generational divide.

The survey also gave those who supported and opposed civic duty voting a list of five possible reasons for why they held their view. They were asked whether a given reason was a "major" reason for their view, a "minor" reason, or "not a reason."

No single major reason for supporting the proposal was predominant. Sixty-nine percent said that one factor was that civic duty voting "would make our government more representative," while 67 percent said they supported it for the philosophical reason that "people have a civic duty to vote." Fifty-six percent said civic duty voting "would increase Americans' confidence in the government," while 55 percent said it "would combat voter suppression."

The one reason that failed to draw majority support for universal civic duty voting was that it "would make it easier for the political party I support to win elections." That was listed as a major reason by just 33 percent, including 28 percent of Democrats and 44 percent of Republicans.

Overwhelmingly, the most important reason for opposition (listed as a major reason by 78 percent of opponents) was a belief that "people have a right not to participate in elections." In addition, 58 percent opposed it because "there are already too many government taxes and fines." These were the only two reasons on the list of five, both of them of a libertarian sort, that drew majorities as major sources of opposition.

The third-most-popular reason for opposition (listed as major by 46 percent) was that a requirement to participate would "disproportionately punish those who already have the hardest time voting." Black Americans and Hispanics were slightly more inclined than whites to list this reason as important, and there was a sharp divide along party lines. Sixty percent of Democratic opponents listed disproportionate punishment as a major reason for their opposition, but only 45 percent of independents and 35 percent of Republicans did so. This finding underscores the importance of accompanying civic duty voting with reforms to make voting easier and more convenient.

Two reasons for opposition were rejected as either minor or not a factor at all: a fear that civic duty voting "would cause too many uneducated people to vote" (listed as a

Table 6: Reasons for Opposing Civic Duty Voting

	Somewhat oppose	Strongly oppose	Total
People have a right to not participate in elections			
Major reason	59%	85%	78%
Minor reason	32	10	15
Not a reason	9	5	6
There are already too many government taxes and fines			
Major reason	45	63	58
Minor reason	35	20	24
Not a reason	21	17	18
It would disproportionately punish those who already have the hardest time voting			
Major reason	44	47	46
Minor reason	36	25	28
Not a reason	20	28	26
It would cause too many uneducated people to vote			
Major reason	26	26	26
Minor reason	31	20	23
Not a reason	43	54	51

	Somewhat oppose	Strongly oppose	Total
It would make it harder for the political party I support to win elections			
Major reason	12	10	10
Minor reason	19	14	15
Not a reason	69	76	74

Respondents to the survey who opposed universal civic duty voting were given a list of possible reasons for their opposition and asked which ones explained their views. This chart shows the differences in reasons given by those who said they were only "somewhat opposed" and those who said they were "strongly opposed."

major reason by only 26 percent of opponents) and a worry that "it would make it harder for the political party I support to win elections" (picked as a major reason by just 10 percent). The former is heartening for "small-d" democrats, the latter a hopeful portent that arguments over civic duty voting need not become mired in our country's partisan polarization—although, again, Trump's radical politicization of voting issues complicates the path of all reformers.

Since the task of persuasion will begin with Americans who are only "somewhat opposed" to civic duty voting, it's worth noting that this group was significantly less likely than those who were "strongly opposed" to offer the two libertarian reasons in explaining their skepticism. Whereas 85 percent of strong opponents listed the right not to participate in elections as a major reason for rejecting the idea, only 59 percent of the somewhat opposed did so. And while 63 percent of strong opponents listed opposition to taxes and fines as an important reason for holding their view, just 45 percent of those somewhat opposed did so. The "moderately opposed" were as worried about punishing those who had the hardest time voting as they were about the taxes and fines themselves.

Advocates of a major reform must be both realistic and hopeful. We are under no illusions that public opinion is, at the moment, on the side of a proposal to require participation in American elections. The idea currently has support from just over a quarter of the American public, and it is strongly opposed by nearly half the country. Advocates of universal civic duty voting have work to do both in answering the arguments made against the idea and in designing its implementation in ways that address the legitimate concerns of those who have doubts that it could work fairly and properly.

We do, however, take heart from the fact that a clear majority of Americans embrace the idea that voting is both a right and a duty. Just as important, about half the country either supports the idea or appears to be open to persuasion. This is not a bad starting point for an idea that has never been advanced in the United States in a systematic way. While its strongest opponents have objections of principle, many less fervent critics are nearly as worried by how it would work in practice—issues that can be addressed by a well-crafted system.

Chapter Seven

Answering the Critics
Responding to Objections to Civic Duty Voting

After President Obama proposed that the United States consider civic duty voting in 2015, critics were quick to voice their dissent.[1] The prominent conservative thinker Jonah Goldberg wrote in *National Review*, "My old boss, William F. Buckley Jr., often said liberals don't care what you do so long as it's compulsory. . . . There's probably no better illustration of this illiberal streak in liberalism than the idea of 'compulsory voting.'"[2]

Others argued that the idea was unconstitutional: "The president apparently does not believe that the right to speak, which is protected under the First Amendment, includes the right not to speak," said the Heritage Foundation's Hans von Spakovsky.[3]

Beyond the constitutional issues discussed earlier, broader objections to civic duty voting go the heart of what it means to be a democracy. Jason Brennan, a Georgetown University political philosopher who is one of the most forceful and articulate foes of compulsory voting, writes that compulsory voting misses the point, which is that we should worry more about the *quality* of the electorate and less about the *quantity* of voters. "If we really want to help America, we shouldn't force citizens to vote," he says. "We should encourage citizens to vote well or not vote at all. Don't ask your neighbor to vote. Instead, ask the ignorant and irrational voters, *how dare you?*"[4]

David Harsanyi, a senior writer for *National Review*, insists that "Mandatory Voting is authoritarian."[5] In a 2016 *Washington Post* piece, he asserted, "We must weed out ignorant Americans from the electorate. . . . [N]ever have so many people with so little knowledge made so many consequential decisions for the rest of us."[6] He drove the point home in a 2020 *National Review* essay: "All mandatory-voting advocates are doing is further degrading the importance of elections and incentivizing more demagoguery. If they truly believed democracy was sacred—rather than a way to accumulate power—they'd want Americans to put more effort in voting for the president than they do in ordering Chinese takeout. And they certainly wouldn't want to force anyone to do it."[7]

Opposition to civic duty voting generally falls into three categories. The most common criticisms involve versions of the libertarian argument against government compulsion— the case made by Goldberg with a light touch, and by Harsanyi with his charge of authoritarianism. The second we might call, in deference to Harsanyi, "the Chinese takeout argument": the fear that civic duty voting would introduce a wave of "ignorant" voters into the electorate. The third reflects practical worries about how civic duty voting would work, particularly if our current voting system were not reformed.

The Argument Against Compulsion

As the Nationscape survey showed, Americans are predisposed to push against anything that smacks of "The government is making you do this." But the civic duty voting requirement we propose would have several options for people who object to voting. Citizens would have the option to mark their ballot "none of the above" (NOTA). They could also submit an entirely blank ballot. Or they could provide some explanation, including conscientious objection, for why they cannot or will not vote. While countries with enforced civic duty voting policies allow for the submission of blank ballots, as we've similarly proposed, providing a NOTA option on the ballot would offer voters an explicit and formal form of abstention.

Nevada enacted a "none of these candidates" option in 1975, and it has been available in state and federal elections since 1976.[8] Since then, the share won by "none of these candidates" in Nevada's presidential elections has ranged from less than half of a percent to 2.56 percent in the 2016 election. A 2019 report on the effects of NOTA found that including a NOTA option "increases participation and reduces the vote shares of non-establishment candidates."[9] The best national example of widespread use of NOTA is in India, where a 2013 Supreme Court decision mandated that a NOTA option be added to all ballots and voting machines. In the first general election after the decision, NOTA votes accounted for 1.1 percent of the total.[10]

A conscientious objection option would further expand the rights of those who do not want to vote. Throughout our history, religious groups such as the Quakers and Mennonites have objected on principle to participating in war—they were often referred to as "the peace churches"—and were granted leave not to fight. During the Vietnam War, conscientious objector status was extended to include many more Americans in other religious denominations as well. We recognize that a minority of Americans may object to participating in the democratic electoral process on principle. The system we propose would grant them comparable conscientious objector status.

But while we hope that this feature will meet and overcome the objections of many critics, we know that a libertarian objection to state compulsion will remain an obstacle for many. Jason Brennan insists that "the side that supports compulsion bears the burden of proof," and he argues that even likely good outcomes, if they can be proven (which he questions), do not necessarily overcome that burden. He also insists that advocates of compulsory participation should acknowledge that skepticism about compulsion is not simply a libertarian concern. It is rooted in the broader liberal tradition. He cites the liberal theorist Gerald Gaus's assertion that "the liberal tradition in political philosophy maintains that each person is free to do as he wishes until some justification is offered for limiting his liberty."[11]

In the interest of a candid debate, we might usefully note at this point that neither of the authors of this book is a libertarian. Our views might fairly be seen as broadly social democratic or liberal (in the New Deal sense of a much-contested word). This means that forms of state action that libertarians might see as interfering with individual liberty we see as advancing it. Regulating the market, protecting the environment, advancing worker rights, establishing social insurance programs and systems of public education, ensuring universal health insurance coverage—all these may involve what libertarians (and many mainstream conservatives) would see as coercion. We would insist that they increase the autonomy and freedom of choice of individuals and their capacity to determine their own course in life. All of which is to argue that since one side's "coercion" can be another side's "liberation," we think the burdens of proof in this debate are equal on both sides.

But we would also argue that conservatives and even

libertarians who might disagree with our politics should consider that the very limited amount of coercion involved in universal civic duty voting—especially since it compels participation but not the actual casting of a vote—is worth engaging in to produce an inclusive polity that would bring the views of all citizens (including libertarians and conservatives) to bear on collective democratic decision-making.

And central to our argument is an insistence that declaring voting a duty is the only sure way to guarantee that the right to vote is fully protected. The country has tried to do this without universal civic duty voting and failed—witness the often violent backlash against the enfranchisement of Black Americans during Reconstruction, leading to the long Jim Crow era, as well as the voter suppression efforts of recent years that culminated in the attack on the Capitol aimed at undoing the outcome of a democratic election. Either we are a democracy or we're not. As a nation, either we believe in full participation or we don't. *The collective decisions a democracy makes should be made by everyone.*

The closest analogue to civic duty voting is jury duty. The obligation to serve on a jury certainly involves compulsion—and, especially for those required to serve on juries for a long trial, it can be a far more onerous form of compulsion that merely asking someone to cast a ballot, filled in or left blank. Yet our nation has rightly accepted the universal obligation to serve on juries as the only way to guarantee fair trials that vindicate the rights of everyone. This is why the end of racial discrimination in the selection of juries—which meant subjecting Black Americans to the *coercive* requirement to serve—was correctly seen by Black Americans as an important advance for liberty as well as fairness. As Justice Thurgood Marshall wrote in *Peters v. Kiff* in 1972: "Illegal and unconstitutional jury selection procedures cast doubt on the integrity of the whole judicial process. They create the appearance of bias in the decision of individual cases, and they increase the risk of actual bias as well."[12] We see a less than universal electorate in a similar light.

Precisely because ending the color bar on jury service provided "a measure of accountability," "fairness," and "integrity for the system of justice," as Charles J. Ogletree Jr., the legendary civil rights lawyer and Harvard Law School professor, wrote, "participation in jury service for all people was, thus, a central victory in the battle for civil rights."[13]

Yes, coercion has its downside, but in the case of jury duty—and, we would insist, voting—the upside is priceless. In his foreword to Andrew Guthrie Ferguson's 2013 book *Why Jury Duty Matters*, Ogletree brought this home: "Today, perhaps as a measure of our progress, all races and all citizens groan equally loudly when the jury summons arrives in the mail. Today, the right to participate occasionally becomes overshadowed with the obligations and inconvenience attendant to the summons. Yet the reason why participation in jury service matters has not changed over the years. The constitutional strength of this country begins with its citizens." Ogletree added: "A jury gives ordinary people extraordinary power."[14] Exactly the same can be said of the right—and the duty—to vote.

The "Ignorant Voters" Argument

Responding to President Obama's suggestion in 2015, Trevor Burrus of the conservative Cato Institute warned Americans to consider that their "fully informed" vote "will count as much as a person who chooses his candidate by throwing a dart at [a] board with all the candidates' pictures."[15] This concern is shared by David Harsanyi and Jason Brennan.

Brennan has written at length about how "voters don't know best," and has argued that citizens lack the specialist "knowledge" required for voting. In *Compulsory Voting: For and Against*, an excellent extended debate between Brennan and compulsory participation advocate Lisa Hill, Brennan argues that compulsory voting "changes the quality of the electorate." The chapter in which he makes this case is entitled "Should We Force the Drunk to Drive?"[16]

At bottom, the argument Brennan makes is an objection to democracy itself—which some on the right have acknowledged with their insistence over the decades that "the United States is a constitutional republic, not a democracy." (We would reply that the United States is, or at least aspires to be, a democratic republic and a constitutional democracy.) Historically, citizens were excluded as "unqualified" to vote on the grounds that they lacked information, education, or a sufficient property stake. But this is precisely the attitude toward voting that the United States has rejected by steadily broadening the franchise, eliminating not only property tests but also poll taxes and "literacy tests." (The scare quotes are appropriate, since the literacy tests were phony, even ridiculous in many of the forms they took, and were typically used in the Jim Crow era to disqualify Black voters but not white voters.)

Brennan, for one, doesn't think much of the electorate that exists *now*, without compulsory voting. He writes that "most voters are already ignorant, biased, economically innumerate, and misinformed." He adds that "the median voter is better informed than the median nonvoter, but not by much."[17] If Brennan's goal, however, is to limit the electorate by rooting out the "ignorant" and the "biased," his problem is not with compulsory voting but with broad democratic participation itself.

An impressive political science literature, from V.O. Key Jr.'s classic *The Responsible Electorate* to Samuel Popkin's more recent *The Reasoning Voter*, argues that voters are more rational in their choices than democracy's critics would suggest. As Key put it in the first sentence of his book:

"The perverse and unorthodox argument of this little book is that voters are not fools."[18] No democratic system—and, for that matter, no governing system—is perfect because, as James Madison memorably observed, human beings are not angels. But liberal democracy works because combining majority rule with guarantees of individual rights has historically done a better job than other regime types in preserving liberty and representing the popular will. The more inclusive electorate that universal civic duty voting would create will better represent the popular will. It's worth noting that this democratic instinct was reflected in the Democracy Fund and UCLA Nationscape survey: even among opponents of civic duty voting, the vast majority *rejected* a fear of "undereducated voters" as a major reason for their view.

Universal voting also stands to *increase* citizen knowledge. It would free up resources now spent on turning out 40 to 60 percent of the electorate, allowing them to be focused instead on the tasks of voter education and persuasion. Civic duty voting would also require candidates and parties to direct their campaigns to the entire electorate, and not simply those on some A-list of "likely" voters. Recall Beazley's observations about the Australian electorate. Voters brought to the polls in Australia by compulsory attendance, who might not otherwise vote, are certainly not as politically attentive as those deeply engaged in politics.

Yet the system itself encourages all citizens to engage, seek information, and make judgments. And the evidence suggests that the additional citizens added to the Australian electorate leaven it; they are wary of political extremes, and, in Beazley's view, increase its "middle class" character while also including the young and the marginalized.

Universal voting could also strengthen the United States' civic culture more broadly and encourage a new commitment to civics education. With voting a requirement for all, high schools would have new incentives to ensure that students receive the requisite tools for active participation in the country's civic life. Other community institutions would have a similar interest. Universal voting would create new opportunities to build a culture of citizenship.

Disparate Effects of Enforcement

Some civil rights and voting rights advocates harbor a well-founded trepidation about monetary penalties for nonvoters. Civic duty voting cannot be isolated from the system within which it operates, and contemporary America's multiplication of fines and fees, disproportionately imposed on low-income communities of color, continues to be a major and unjust burden. Monetary penalties for nonvoting therefore have the potential for disparate negative impacts on precisely the vulnerable groups civic duty voting seeks to empower. Our proposal for civic duty voting addresses these concerns. It includes a variety of protections and options to keep the burdens of the fine to a minimum, to make failure to vote noncriminal, to ensure that any fines are not compounded with interest or penalties, to allow any fines to be waived easily, and to give nonvoters easy alternatives to paying the fine.

Automatic voter registration—which we support—when combined with universal civic duty voting, introduces another challenge of particular concern to leaders in the Latinx, Asian American, Pacific Islander, and Native American communities. Under an automatic registration policy, noncitizens could be accidentally registered to vote, through no action of their own.[19] Confirming eligibility to vote is essential to the policy design of automatic voter registration, but states must also put protections in place for noncitizens inadvertently added to the electoral rolls through such a program. The goal is to ensure that they are not considered guilty of fraudulent voting or attempting to vote, unless they willfully attempt to vote despite being aware of their ineligibility. Similarly, any civic duty voting policy must also provide that those erroneously added to the electoral rolls are not penalized for failing to vote.

The purpose of civic duty voting is to increase participation, not to lay traps for voters or to penalize vulnerable communities. Mitigating the possible disparate effects of the policy must be a top priority. Communities that have been historically marginalized and those that have been discouraged or blocked from voting in the past have reason to be concerned that a process requiring citizens to vote could be used against them. For this reason, it is critical that a civic duty voting requirement be enacted in tandem with other reforms to the voting system.

Chapter Eight

Paving the Way for Universal Voting
The Urgency of Gateway Reforms

Universal civic duty voting is a logical leap forward from the Voting Rights Act of 1965—and from any new and much-needed protections to the right to vote. Our proposal is designed to vindicate the liberating purposes of the 1965 law and the rights guaranteed in the Fourteenth and Fifteenth Amendments of the Constitution. When the United States Supreme Court gutted key provisions of the Voting Rights Act in *Shelby County v. Holder*, as we have noted already, it unleashed a new wave of voter suppression, rolling back advances once thought secure. A vibrant democracy movement, in turn, pushed back against the vote suppressors and worked actively for reforms that would *increase* participation.

A demand for universal civic duty voting is also a demand for such reforms, which would put an end to the cycles of inclusion and exclusion that have been part of our nation's story from the beginning. As our polling has shown, many Americans worry that civic duty voting will not work unless it is implemented along with other changes to our system. We agree. A range of gateway reforms is inextricably linked to the successful introduction of universal participation.

The example of Australia is again instructive: that country's system works well because the requirement to vote works in tandem with a range of voter-friendly policies. Election day is conveniently scheduled on a Saturday, for example. Registration and access to the ballot are made easy, and election officials are required to make energetic, affirmative outreach efforts to ensure that citizens are registered. Voting opportunities, including mail-in voting, early voting, and numerous polling places, are extensive. Because everyone must vote, the practice of intimidating people at polling places so they won't vote is nonexistent. And the country's system of election administration is nonpartisan and professional, reducing the opportunities and temptations to tilt rules and practices in favor of one side.

The reforms we propose build on the work of the voting rights and democracy movements, and they should be promoted by federal law. Gateway reforms fall into three categories: expanding opportunities to register, increasing the options for voting, and strengthening effective election administration.

Expanding Opportunities to Register
Same-Day Voter Registration

Historically, the requirement to register in advance of voting was enacted as an intentional hurdle to participation, targeting the influx of immigrants in the late nineteenth and early twentieth centuries while also preventing the extension of the right to vote for Black Americans. It has also for years been standard practice to rationalize deadlines cutting off registration well before election day as necessary to give election officials time to create accurate lists of eligible voters.

But technological advances and the digitization of voting rolls make this rationale for advanced registration anachronistic. Same-day registration encourages new voters to enter the process, and also allows existing voters to update or correct errors in their registrations. The procedure, first adopted in the mid-1970s in Maine, Minnesota, and Wisconsin, has consistently led to significant increases in voter participation, without any major problems of implementation. The number of states that offer same-day registration has grown dramatically. In 2020, twenty-one states and the District of Columbia offered people the opportunity to use it, and it made a difference; consistent with earlier studies, states with same-day registration had turnout rates 5 percent higher than states without it.

Automatic Voter Registration

Twenty states and the District of Columbia have adopted policies that automatically register citizens to vote and update an existing voter registration whenever a citizen interacts with the state Department of Motor Vehicles and, in some jurisdictions, other governmental or social service agencies that collect citizenship information. Citizens typically are given the opportunity to opt out of registering, rather than being required to opt in. Oregon was the first state to move away from the opt-in model when the state implemented automatic registration in 2016. In that year alone, more than 225,000 residents were automatically registered through Oregon's Department of Motor Vehicles. The process, still relatively new, has rapidly expanded. In cases where ineligible voters (such as noncitizens) are mistakenly added to the rolls, states should enact "safe harbor" provisions to protect those added to the rolls by mistake. California and Vermont have such provisions to protect noncitizens in the small number of cases where this has taken place. Since immigration is a federal responsibility, Congress should enact national protections along these lines as well.

Restoring the Right to Vote for Citizens with Felony Convictions

Nearly all states, thanks to significant progress achieved over the last decade, now allow citizens with felony convictions to have their voting rights restored after completion of their sentence. However, the policies concerning the way that probation, parole, and the payment of fines and fees are handled vary considerably across states, as the

Florida battle showed. Entirely decoupling people's right to vote from their incarceration status—as Maine, Vermont, and Washington, D.C., have done—would be a major step forward. At a minimum, a uniform standard that provides full restoration of voting rights after a person's release from prison would remove this functionally and historically racist barrier to voting.

Online Registration

Forty states and the District of Columbia now allow people to register online. This cost-saving measure, first implemented in Arizona in 2002, has eased voting registration for many.[1] The COVID-19 pandemic gave additional impetus for online registration, as options for in-person registration narrowed in 2020.

Preregistration of 16- and 17-Year-Olds

Twenty-three states now allow eligible young people to preregister before they are eighteen years old. Their names are then automatically placed on the electoral rolls upon their eighteenth birthday. Preregistration allows schools the opportunity to engage and educate students in civics and voting in high school, before they disperse to the workforce or to college. Some studies have shown that this early registration makes it more likely that young people will become voters when they reach voting age.[2]

Expanding Options for Voting

States have also made significant progress since the days when voting was largely restricted to the first Tuesday after the first Monday in November—a vestige of a federal law enacted in 1845 based on the needs of farmers in what was then a heavily agricultural nation. The election of 2020, in which an astonishing 111 million people voted by means other than in person on that second Tuesday, shows just how far we have come from that anachronistic concept of voting.

Early Voting

Forty-three states and the District of Columbia now allow people to vote before election day.[3] A recent study on the impact of early voting in Ohio found "substantial positive impacts of early voting on turnout, equal to 0.22 percentage points of additional turnout per additional early voting day."[4] In the 2020 election, 25 percent of voters cast their votes early in person.

The number of days that early voting is permitted and how convenient the process is made vary greatly between states. For example, early voting in Florida must begin at least ten days before an election, while Virginia enacted a law in the 2020 legislative session allowing forty-five days of early voting. Expanded early voting was also one of the successful adaptations made during the COVID-19 crisis. Federal policies to require states to offer at least fifteen days of early voting would be an important step in the right direction.

Vote-by-Mail

Expanding mail-in voting was a central focus of efforts to allow people to vote safely in the 2020 elections. In addition, many states sent ballot applications, or ballots themselves, to every voter in their jurisdictions. Although most states initially made the expansions applicable only for the pandemic year, a number of states have moved to make the expansion permanent. Sixteen states, either by legislation or in their state constitutions, still require voters to provide an excuse in order to vote by absentee. They should join the other twenty-nine states and the District of Columbia in the move toward no-excuse absentee voting. Five states—Colorado, Hawaii, Oregon, Utah, and Washington—have gone beyond no-excuse absentee ballots by sending ballots to all or almost all eligible voters. California did the same for the 2020 election, as did Montana, Nevada, New Jersey, Vermont, and the District of Columbia. The results of the mail voting expansion were dramatic. Forty-five percent of all voters voted by mail. While all states had increases in turnout compared to 2016, the states that had full or

close-to-full voting by mail had a 9 percent increase in turnout, compared to a 5 percent increase in states that did not
do so. Expanded mail-in voting should clearly be a permanent part of our election process.

Flexible Election Day Options

During the pandemic, many states invested in innovative
efforts to make polling places safe. These efforts would be
equally useful in a nation free of COVID-19. Curbside voting is one example: poll workers took ballots or portable
machines to voters' cars, eliminating the need to stand on
line. Some jurisdictions used mobile voting centers. The use
of drop boxes grew dramatically, for both early and election
day voting. It also seems obvious that the successes during
the pandemic in recruiting and training a new generation of
election workers should be replicated in calmer times. Widely
available early voting also improves the experience for election day voters by reducing the number of voters who need
to use a single polling place. The shortened lines and wait
times achieved in 2020 should be the goal for every election.

Convenient Placement of Accessible Precincts and Vote Centers

The success of universal voting will also depend on the
convenient placement of polling places and the effective
use of vote centers. This can be especially important for

rural and Indigenous voters who often need to travel long distances to cast a ballot—particularly in tribal lands, where access is now often severely limited. Quantity matters: all jurisdictions should place precincts and vote centers in enough places to ensure ease of voting for all citizens.

Voters with disabilities can have their right to vote impaired when voting sites lack wheelchair accessibility or present other physical challenges All voting centers should meet Americans with Disabilities Act requirements and allow people with disabilities maximum access and privacy in their voting process. Colorado currently conducts and releases audits that detail counties' compliance with federal accessibility standards in their polling places after each election, and the rest of the country should follow suit.

All these reforms make sense with or without universal civic duty voting. But a system that would require everyone to vote must do all it can to remove obstacles to citizens carrying out their responsibilities.

Effective Election Administration

Even good election policies can be undermined if election administration does not inspire confidence among voters that their participation is valued and that their votes will count. Election administration had not been a topic that made anyone's heart beat faster, yet one heartening result of the 2020 pandemic election was the transformation of many election officials into national heroes. Like other essential workers—for essential they were—they deserved the acclaim. The honor we accorded them should inspire far more interest in the measures we need to take to administer elections professionally and effectively, another essential step toward universal civic duty voting. As we noted at the outset, laws in some states to undercut the nonpartisan administration of elections must be challenged both through federal legislation and in the courts. Election subversion has become as significant a threat to voting rights as voter suppression.

Maintenance of Voting Lists

Every jurisdiction must maintain accurate and up-to-date voting lists. Even with civic duty voting in place, it will be necessary to guard against overly aggressive purging policies, which often remove eligible voters from the electoral rolls. Aggressive purges have resulted in major legal battles in a number of states, as recounted earlier. States should carefully follow the list management procedures specified in the National Voter Registration Act and engage in careful cross-state cooperation through the Electronic Registration Information Center.

Adequate Funding of Election Administration

The funding of elections became a major issue during the COVID-19 crisis, and substantial federal support on an ongoing basis will be required to make voting accessible to all citizens. Elections are typically an afterthought in local budgeting. This must change. Together, all levels of government must come to see investments in the election process as critical investments in democracy itself.

Building on 2020

The registration and voting reforms advanced by organizers, advocates, and forward-looking election officials are encouraging and important. They have had real effects on turnout. Expanded voting opportunities in blue, red, and purple states are positive steps toward increased participation. Embracing and building on these achievements—and, yes, resisting efforts to roll them back—will improve American democracy now, and give universal civic duty voting its best opportunity to succeed.

Chapter Nine

Getting from Here to There
How to Implement Universal Voting

All proponents of large reforms face two basic questions: How will it work? How do you get it enacted? For many, requiring all Americans to vote seems a radical idea. We have tried to persuade readers that it is no more radical than jury duty, and that it has been fully tested in two dozen countries. Australia, a country with a democratic system similar to ours in many ways, provides more than adequate proof of concept. Nearly a hundred years of experience there suggests that there is nothing half-baked or reckless in asking every citizen to participate in choosing their elected leaders.

And especially when it comes to voting rights, practices that once seemed radical can quickly become the norm once they are adopted. The secret ballot was not commonly used in the United States until the last decade of the nineteenth century. Now we can't imagine voting in any other way. Extending the right to vote beyond white men with property once seemed radical too.

It's always fair to ask reformers: what problem are you trying to remedy? The United States has struggled for equality of participation from the beginning, and progress toward inclusion has faced resistance again and again. Declaring voting a civic duty by law declares that everyone counts—and that everyone has a responsibility to be counted.

The grave challenges to our democracy reflected in former President Trump's systematic lies about the outcome of the 2020 election and dramatized by the violent assault on our nation's Capitol also argue for a full-fledged reset. Trump was able to exploit the uncertainties of our registration and voting system to incite suspicions among his followers that the other side had cheated. The instability and lack of uniformity in state laws around voting fed his demagoguery. In response, the nation should firmly and unequivocally declare that voting rights will never again be subjected to the whims of temporary majorities. Recognizing the obligation of every citizen to participate in our democracy offers a comprehensive way to put the chaos behind us. No more voter suppression, no more purging of the rolls, no more disqualifications for "mismatched" signatures, no more invalidated ballots, no more voter intimidation, no more resigned apathy—everyone votes! It is—or it certainly should be—the American way.

We are inspired by Abraham Lincoln's 1862 declaration: "The dogmas of the quiet past are inadequate to the stormy present. The occasion is piled high with difficulty, and we must rise with the occasion. As our case is new, so we must think anew, and act anew. We must disenthrall ourselves, and then we shall save our country."[1]

So how might we act anew? What precisely must we do?

The core feature of universal civic duty voting is that participation in significant general elections at the federal, state, municipal, and county levels should be made a requirement for every eligible citizen in the United States. This raises two further questions: How would governments—federal, state, and municipal—implement the policy? And what strategies can supporters use to advance the idea by persuading fellow citizens and legislators?

Implementing Universal Civic Duty Voting

Civic duty voting, and the legislation to enact the policy at each level of government, will vary significantly based on the level of government seeking to adopt it, and on the laws and constitutional dictates in each jurisdiction. Crafting appropriate language will be a task for bill writers and election officials. But certain fundamentals should shape any legislation.

Universal civic duty voting should be put in place for all major general elections. Achieving this goal will require steps at every level of government. Many states and localities hold elections every year involving combinations of national, state, and local offices; different gradual paths are possible toward having civic duty voting implemented in these scenarios. The first steps may involve local experiments with municipal elections, or statewide experiments in gubernatorial elections. In the course of adopting universal civic duty voting, some states might choose to consolidate elections to hold fewer of them. But the goal should be to have citizens take on this basic civic responsibility at every level of government, and to enact election laws and shape approaches to election administration that make voting as simple and easy as possible.

It's true that in some jurisdictions with strong inclinations toward one party or the other, primaries can determine who will ultimately hold office. We have not included primaries under our proposal because eligibility rules in primaries are complicated and vary from state to state. For example, some states do not allow "independent" or "no party declared" voters to cast ballots in primaries. It would, however, be wise for states with primaries open to all voters to apply civic duty voting to both the first round and runoffs. In any event, we would hope and expect that civic duty voting, and the complementary reforms that would accompany it, will encourage broader participation in primaries by making all forms of voting easier and more accessible.

As we have stressed throughout, the fine for not voting should be small—no more than $20. It should not be subject to increases through penalty fees or accrued interest, and it should not be the basis for criminal enforcement under any circumstances. Jurisdictions can offer an hour or two of community service as an alternative penalty in lieu of the fine. Jurisdictions should phase in the system gradually. A phase-in could include the use of warnings, rather than fines, for the first election requiring voting, and a warning rather than a fine could be used as a penalty for a non-voter's first infraction once the system is fully in place. No one should be denied government services or benefits for not participating in an election, as is the practice in some countries with the system. The goal is not to penalize but to create a culture of participation by raising our expectations of citizens.

Jurisdictions should also consider creating voting incentives for eligible citizens. Many proponents of universal participation are drawn to the idea of an incentive-based system rather than an enforcement-based requirement. While the notion is attractive, the experience of other countries, as we have shown, suggests that education and messaging about voting as a civic duty, along with a light-touch enforcement mechanism, produce better results. Nevertheless, jurisdictions might offer a variety of individual and community-based incentives, which could increase compliance.

For example, citizens who vote could receive discounted public fees for licenses or other municipal services. Many municipalities have various forms of tax credits, for people with limited incomes or for senior citizens; one could imagine a refundable civic participation tax credit as well as a lottery for those who participate in the election. As we noted earlier, however, there may be legal impediments to incentives. State and federal laws should be clarified so that such incentives cannot be interpreted as "bribery" or "vote buying."

In any state or municipality adopting universal civic duty voting, an official or agency would be designated as having the responsibility to design and implement the program. In many states, the secretary of state is the chief election official; elsewhere it is a board of elections or other body. Legislation should designate the official or agency with clear responsibility for implementing the various aspects of the program, including coordinating the different entities whose participation would be required. The responsibilities should include an energetic public education effort, beginning well before any enforcement begins to take place.

After an election has been completed, the administering agency should send eligible voters who did not participate a letter, including a list of the acceptable reasons for not participating, and asking them to specify a reason. Additional forms of communication such as emails and texts can be used as documentation. Once adequate and earnest communication efforts have been made, and if there is no response, the small fine or other enforcement options would be assessed.

Acceptable reasons for not voting should be established in the legislation and clearly communicated. An Australian judge summarized his view of adequate reasons this way:

> Physical obstruction, whether of sickness or outside prevention, or of natural events, or accident of any kind, would certainly be recognized by law in such a case. One might also imagine cases where an intending voter on his way to the poll was diverted to save life, or to prevent crime, or to assist at some great disaster, such as a fire; in all of which cases, in my opinion, the law would recognize the competitive claims of public duty.[2]

Perhaps certain work responsibilities should be included as well. In the spirit of light-touch enforcement, election officials should give the benefit of the doubt to the nonvoter in assessing penalties. But giving voters every opportunity to vote in a convenient way should allow most Americans to avoid all but the most unpredictable diversions from performance of their duty.

One important acceptable reason for not participating should be clearly spelled out: citizens with a conscientious or religious objection to voting should be able to apply for a permanent exemption on these grounds. Again the presumption would be in favor of granting an exemption. In addition, as discussed earlier, voters will have the option of casting a blank ballot as well as choosing an explicit "none of the above" option on the ballots themselves. Every possible step should be taken to ensure that civic duty voting cannot in any way be construed as "coerced speech." This is important for constitutional reasons, as we showed in Chapter Five, but it is also a response to the legitimate libertarian concerns.

Legislation should be carefully tailored to provide access for all communities and to protect against misuse or unintended negative consequences. It should include provisions for language minorities, for people with disabilities, for voting by tribal communities, and for ensuring that noncitizens and people with felony convictions are protected from penalty if they are mistakenly and unknowingly registered or required to vote.

The increased turnout achieved by universal voting will generate greater fixed and variable costs. Adequate funding for election administration to cover the costs of higher turnout is essential to the successful implementation of civic duty voting. This is a responsibility for all levels of government—local, state, and federal. Budgets should include recruitment and adequate training for election administrative staff, and for a diverse, bilingual, younger, and better-paid set of workers for additional early, mail, and election day voting. Funding should also be sufficient for updated voting machinery for precincts and vote centers, for the sorting equipment necessary for expanded mail voting, for an expansion in the number of polling places where necessary, and for a large-scale public education effort.

In addition to disseminating information about candidates and ballot questions, voter communications must clearly explain the details of how and where voters can cast a ballot. Officials can use a number of channels to inform voters of their responsibilities: public service announcements, social media, public agency postings, notices in schools and libraries, comprehensive mailings, political parties and candidate campaigns, civic and religious institutions, and nonprofit organizations. Effective designs for marketing and outreach matter: all of these efforts should use communications outlets and mechanisms trusted in varied communities, and all materials should be available in multiple relevant languages. The voter education program should make special efforts to reach out to young and first-time voters. Expanding civic education in schools and recruiting young people to serve as poll workers would be important in broadening engagement.

Schools should expand civic education. Civics education should be a curricular requirement in every school district. In light of the spread of misinformation and disinformation, "media literacy" programs should be part of a comprehensive civic education curriculum.

Universal civic duty voting can begin at any of our three levels of government. While the underlying principles are the same for each of them, they have distinct responsibilities.

What the Federal Government Should Do

Enact Legislation Adopting Universal Civic Duty Voting for All Federal Elections

While Congress cannot mandate election procedures for state and municipal elections, the Constitution's elections clause gives the federal government the authority to require that all citizens participate in federal elections, which take place every two years. While the adoption of civic duty voting for federal offices—presidential, Senate, and House elections—would not automatically require states to follow suit, it is likely that most if not all states would conform their state election procedures to the federal standards to avoid having different rules affecting the same voters at the same election.

Restore and Update the Voting Rights Act

The success of universal civic duty voting depends on laws that protect voting rights and ease participation. As the success of the original Voting Rights Act demonstrated, there is no adequate substitute for robust federal legislation to protect the right to vote, block voter suppression, and prevent election subversion. Despite the Supreme Court's shameful July 2021 decision in *Brnovich v Democratic National Committee* further eviscerating the 1965 law, the Justice Department should aggressively monitor changes in election laws and act wherever and whenever it can to protect the voting rights of all.[3]

Strengthen Federal Authority to Set Standards and Modernize Election Administration

Congress should substantially expand the authority and funding of the Election Assistance Commission, giving it the ability to set national standards for election administration, maintain effective administration, and ensure voting access and integrity. The voters of the United States deserve the kind of competent national election administration that exists in virtually every other advanced democracy. The federal government, as we've noted, should revise bribery and vote-buying statutes to permit governmentally sponsored and uniformly applied incentives for voting. The federal government should finance any transition costs these policies might impose.

Mandate Employers to Give Employees Paid Time Off for Voting and Civic Participation

A civic duty voting program would heighten the need for employers to offer paid time off for employees to fulfill their requirement to vote. Employers should be required to allow employees to work at the polls and in election offices at election time as well. While there is considerable disagree-ment among voting rights advocates about whether election day should be moved to the weekend or declared a holiday, the nation does need a robust debate on whether the "first Tuesday after the first Monday in November" date is condu-cive to maximum participation. Fortunately, the widespread availability of mail-in and early voting takes substantial pres-sure off election day itself, as the experience of 2020 showed.

What State Governments Should Do

Pass State Legislation Adopting Universal Civic Duty Voting

All states should pass legislation requiring voting as a uni-versal civic duty for all general state elections, based on the implementation principles outlined above. As a helpful starting point, Appendix A offers the text of a civic duty voting bill introduced in 2021 in Connecticut by State Sena-tor Will Haskell.

Pass Enabling Legislation for Municipalities

Where required, states should pass legislation—and, if neces-sary, constitutional amendments—enabling all counties and municipalities to enact universal civic duty voting for local elections. In states that do not adopt the system statewide, advocates of civic duty voting should press for local option laws that give counties and localities the power to apply the requirement to vote to their citizens for all elections.

Enact the Set of Complementary Gateway Reforms That Enable Successful Implementation

States should enact a full suite of registration and voting reforms to remove barriers, increase voter registration, and make it as simple as possible for eligible citizens to vote. They should also enact their own statewide voting rights laws, as Virginia did in 2021.

Advocate for Federal Legislation

States should advocate for the passage of universal civic duty voting at the federal level, and for full federal funding of broadened elections. Governors and state election officials have significant influence with their congressional delegations; they should use it on behalf of full participation.

What County, City, and Town Governments Should Do

Advocate for Passage of Federal and State Legislation Creating Universal Civic Duty Voting, and for Enabling Legislation for Local Jurisdictions

Working with other municipalities and civic organizations, municipal officials who want to adopt civic duty voting can take a leadership role in urging Congress and the states to adopt the policy for all federal and statewide general elections. Where it is not possible to win statewide enactment of civic duty voting, municipalities can advocate for their state to adopt proper enabling legislation, if existing home rule legislation is insufficient.

Create a Municipal Program of Universal Civic Duty Voting

Counties, cities, and other local jurisdictions with appropriate legal authorization should create municipal programs analogous to the state programs proposed earlier, designing appropriate enforcement mechanisms. Deciding which elections civic duty voting should apply to, and whether consolidation of elections is possible, would be an important set of decisions for local governments to make.

Recruit, Train, and Fairly Compensate Election Workers

The lack of effective and properly trained election workers has been a consistent challenge to reliable election administration. This was a major challenge that was met effectively in 2020. Energetic recruitment of workers, including students, the young, and people fluent in languages other than English, should be prioritized. AmeriCorps and other service programs can be mobilized as part of this effort. Adequate pay and manageable working shifts are important for election worker recruitment and retention. As the size and diversity of the participating electorate increase and computerized processes become the norm, mandatory and modernized training of poll and precinct workers is critical as well.

As this chapter has suggested, civic duty voting has a double benefit. It works on its own to create a broad and inclusive electorate. But it also makes us think far more about the importance of elections and how they work. It is a prod for creativity, reform, and innovation in legislation and administration. A debate about the specific idea of universal voting would be the catalyst for a much larger conversation about democracy.

Chapter Ten

From the Impossible to the Inevitable
A Strategy for Universal Participation

What could more profoundly vindicate the idea of America than plain and humble people—unsung, the downtrodden, the dreamers not of high station, not born to wealth or privilege, not of one religious tradition but many, coming together to shape their country's course? . . . What greater form of patriotism is there than the belief that America is not yet finished, that we are strong enough to be self-critical, that each successive generation can look upon our imperfections and decide that it is in our power to remake this nation to more closely align with our highest ideals. . . . What's our excuse today for not voting? How do we so casually discard the right for which so many fought? How do we so fully give away our power, our voice, in shaping America's future?

—*President Barack Obama, March 7, 2015, in Selma, Alabama, marking the fiftieth anniversary of "Bloody Sunday"*

Enacting a major reform requires persuasion, organizing, and persistence. It often entails moving new ideas from the category of the impossible to the realm of the inevitable. This book—and the working group report from which it grew—can be seen as the beginning of that effort. The reformer's task involves responding to doubts, explaining advantages, pointing to successful models, and reassuring those who fear the unintended consequences of change. This means showing how a new initiative can achieve long-standing objectives and is legitimately part of a long historical tradition. President Obama's Selma speech was powerful precisely because it so eloquently invoked the great and honorable trajectory of American self-criticism and self-correction.

A large innovation can also become possible when it is seen as the right response to a particular moment. The election of 2020—with its unprecedented challenges to voting and its striking level of controversy and conflict—has already triggered a sweeping inquiry into the state of elections in the United States. The global threat to democracy makes this debate all the more urgent. Universal civic duty voting meets the conversation where it is and points to a way out of our cul-de-sacs.

If some ideas catch on quickly, others require a longer gestation period, a chance to prove themselves—what the great social thinker Max Weber called "a strong and slow boring of hard boards." In the United States, our federal system has encouraged experiments at the state and local levels that, when successful, culminated in durable national change. The "states' rights" slogan has been regularly invoked in our history by conservatives and reactionaries to defend the privileges of local oligarchies (including slaveholders). But state innovation has also been a progressive hallmark, as Justice Brandeis's encouragement to states to "try novel social and economic experiments" brought home.[1] Brandeis's "laboratories of democracy" were particularly fruitful during the Progressive Era, when successful reforms at the state level culminated in national programs during the New Deal.

At times, ideas initially rejected nationally get picked up by states and then circulate back to the national discussion—consider, for example, state leadership, particularly in California, on the climate question. In the case of political reforms, same-day registration was first passed in Maine, Minnesota, and Wisconsin in the 1970s. President Jimmy Carter and Vice President Walter Mondale tried and failed to pass election day registration in Congress in 1977. It was considered for inclusion in the National Voter Registration Act of 1993 but dropped because of conservative opposition. Nonetheless, it continued to spread from state to state, to the point that by 2020, twenty-one states and the District of Columbia embraced the system. Same-day registration became one of the core provisions of the For the People Act.

Ranked-choice voting, also known as the instant-runoff system, has had a similar trajectory. Instead of voting for a single candidate, voters rank their choices. The ballots cast for candidates with the fewest first-place votes are redistributed to a voter's second choice. The process continues until one candidate wins a majority. Ranked-choice voting was first used in a few municipalities in a few states as a way to cut the costs of runoff elections and to prevent elections from being marred by independent or third-party "spoilers." Under various iterations, the system can also help ensure that minority communities win representation in legislative bodies.

Promoted for years by Fair Vote and other election reform organizations, the system of ranked-choice voting has recently begun to win favor at the state level. Maine adopted ranked-choice voting by referendum in 2016. Although a ranked-choice voting initiative failed in Massachusetts in 2020, the system was adopted through a successful ballot initiative in Alaska as part of a wider set of voter reforms. In 2019, voters in New York City adopted ranked-choice voting for local elections. It was first used citywide in primaries and elections for mayor and other offices in 2021.

Universal civic duty voting can follow a similar path. The idea has already begun to enter the mainstream conversation, as evidenced by President Obama's public support for it in 2015. The concept is gradually becoming a standard item on lists of potential reforms to improve the nation's voting system. A January 2021 *Washington Post* editorial, for example, urged President Biden "to convene a high-level commission to recommend a democracy overhaul," suggesting that it "could even review how mandatory voting has worked in places such as Australia."[2] The idea will have become truly mainstream when editorial writers don't feel obligated to introduce it with the word "even."

That will happen when advocates and organizations engaged in the work of voting rights and democracy reform embrace the idea. And they are starting to do so. Supporters of civic duty voting now include the NAACP, Dēmos, State Voices, and Community Change, and the concept is on the agenda for discussion at other organizations as well. Like every policy expanding voter registration and voting, universal civic duty voting will require grassroots support and engagement to win serious consideration at all levels of government.

And as with all ideas a few steps ahead of the conventional wisdom, universal civic duty voting will have to be taken up by legislators with the courage to introduce a proposal that, for now (as our own polling showed), is not yet popular but has potential to win wider support. Here again, the recent track record is encouraging for mainstreaming voting ideas that seemed, only a decade or so ago, marginal and adventurous; many of these are now part of the suite of reforms that should accompany and bolster civic duty voting. Oregon adopted all-mail voting through a 1998 citizens' initiative, and in the 2000 election it became the first state to implement the system. Washington State began using all-mail voting in 2012, and Colorado joined two years later. In 2020, six additional states plus Washington, D.C., mailed ballots directly to voters.

Despite the efforts to roll back mail voting in roughly a dozen Republican states, voters with a wide range of political views welcomed the convenience of mail voting. More generally, states that adopted all or most of the reforms that are "gateways" and prerequisites for successful implementation of universal voting have shown that they work. Minnesota, Colorado, Maine, Wisconsin, and Washington are among them, and these states had turnout levels respectively of 80.0 percent, 76.4 percent, 76.3 percent, 75.8 percent, and 75.7 percent in the 2020 elections.

In Connecticut in 2021, State Senator Will Haskell, the vice chair of the Government Administration and Elections Committee, took a major step by introducing a universal civic duty voting bill. While the bill failed, Haskell courageously broke the policy ice. Other legislators have an experience to build on. Shortly thereafter, State Representative Dylan Fernandes introduced a universal civic duty voting bill in Massachusetts.

As with instant runoffs, municipalities may be the prime

movers in adopting civic duty voting. This could create a powerful dynamic. If, for example, a blue city in a purple state adopted the system not only for municipal elections but state elections as well, it would immediately magnify the city's influence in state elections. In an important 2015 article in *The Atlantic*, Harvard law professor Nicholas Stephanopoulos described what could happen next:

> At this point, redder jurisdictions would face enormous pressure to follow the blue city's lead. Not doing so would award the Democrats an electoral bonanza: a surge in turnout in their urban stronghold unmatched by greater participation in suburbs and exurbs. To get a sense of how strong the Republicans' incentive would be, think back to the 2000 and 2004 presidential elections, both of which came down to a single swing state. Bush prevailed in Florida and again in Ohio. But he likely *wouldn't* have won if Miami and Columbus had required all their eligible voters to go to the polls.
>
> Importantly, it's easier for a single city to adopt compulsory voting than for myriad suburbs and exurbs to follow suit. This collective action problem is why compulsory voting probably wouldn't stay at the local level for long.

Red states, in particular, would find it in their interest to impose statewide voting mandates. By requiring *all* eligible voters to participate, they would stop a few blue municipalities from benefiting at the expense of the many red ones. And once red states jumped on the bandwagon, it's unlikely that blue states—or the federal government—would lag far behind.[3]

Stephanopoulos is not naive. He notes, for example, that red state governments could try to ban municipal experiments with civic duty voting—and we've stressed that some state constitutions give localities far more leeway than others. Nonetheless, as Stephanopoulos argues, courts have often looked askance at state efforts "to eliminate local policies aimed at increasing turnout." His conclusion: "Compulsory voting . . . is not as far-fetched an idea as it might seem. For it to take root in America, all that's necessary is for a single city (in the right state) to take the plunge."

In the wake of the 2020 presidential election, civic duty voting is anything but far-fetched. It provides our nation with the best path to full inclusion of all our citizens in the democratic project and could serve as a powerful spur to the reforms we need to defend and advance our democracy.

Chapter Eleven

Securing Rights, Embracing Responsibilities

"When you see something that is not right, you must say something. You must do something." The words are those of John Lewis in his final message to the world in an essay published shortly after his death in the *New York Times*. He continued: "Democracy is not a state. It is an act, and each generation must do its part to help build what we called the Beloved Community, a nation and world society at peace with itself."[1]

In a few words, Lewis spoke large truths about democracy: that a commitment to it must be active, not passive, and that the struggle for it must be ongoing.

Lewis devoted his life to making our country more democratic, and to a vision of democracy that was at once demanding and serene, radical in its hopes and moderate in its spirit. We have a great distance to go to reach the destination Lewis envisioned for our nation.

The idea of making universal civic duty voting a reality in the United States does not rest on a utopian claim that this single reform would miraculously heal all that ails American democracy. Political scientists Steven Levitsky and Daniel Ziblatt, among others, have pointed to the powerfully anti-majoritarian aspects of our political system. In an essay published in the *New York Times* shortly before the 2020 election, they wrote, "Democracy is supposed to be a game of numbers: The party with the most votes wins. In our political system, however, the majority does not govern. Constitutional design and recent political geographic trends—where Democrats and Republicans live—have unintentionally conspired to produce what is effectively becoming minority rule."[2]

In 2016, Trump won a majority in the Electoral College while losing the popular vote to Hillary Clinton by 2.9 million ballots. In 2020, the winner of the popular vote did prevail, but it was a close call. While Joe Biden won by more than 7 million votes nationwide, his combined margins of victory in the states of Wisconsin, Arizona, and Georgia totaled just under 43,000 votes. In the second Congressional district of Nebraska, which awards electors both statewide and by congressional district, Biden won an additional elector by around 22,000 votes. Thus, a flip of about 32,000 votes would have given the overwhelming loser of the popular vote a two vote Electoral College margin—and reelection.

The U.S. Senate is also structured in a deeply anti-majoritarian way. After the Democrats' Georgia runoff victories in 2021, the Senate is now split fifty-fifty. But the fifty Democratic senators represent 41 million more Americans than the fifty Republican senators. This is no surprise, since Wyoming, with 582,000 people, has the same representation as California, with close to 40 million. With the filibuster rule, senators representing roughly a fifth of the nation's population can, in theory at least, block the will of those representing the overwhelming majority of Americans.

The makeup of the Supreme Court is, bluntly, determined by who happens to die when, who happens to be president at the time, and which party happens to control the Senate. Control of the Court has been a passionate political question for half a century, and the increasing polarization of politics affects the Court no less than any other institution. The raw, abusive politics involved in Senate Republican leader Mitch McConnell's blockade against Merrick Garland, President Obama's 2016 nominee to the Court, underscored the bitterness and undercut the Court's legitimacy. And under Trump, as Levitsky and Ziblatt point out, "Neil Gorsuch and Brett Kavanaugh became the first two Supreme Court justices in history to be appointed by a president who lost the popular vote and then be confirmed by senators who represented less than half the electorate."[3] In 2020, Amy Coney Barrett became the third.

With conservatives in control, the Supreme Court has been an active agent in making the United States less democratic.

Nothing better illustrates the Roberts Court's anti-democratic tenor than the *Shelby v. Holder* decision undercutting the Voting Rights Act, considered in tandem with the *Citizens United v. FEC* ruling. The latter dramatically expanded the ways that organized corporate money can flow into the political process by allowing corporations and other outside groups to spend unlimited amounts of money on elections.[4] *Citizens United*, in particular, underscored the interaction between rising economic inequality over the last forty years and rising political inequality. The decline in living standards for millions of Americans came after many years during which conservatives demonized government. This produced an ironic vicious cycle, as many voters with the greatest stake in public action to right economic imbalances lost faith in government's capacity to act at all. The ensuing politics of obstruction meant that the government failed to take the very steps that might have restored public confidence in its capacities.

Imbalances of wealth have spilled over into the political process. These have been partly abated by a surge in small-dollar fundraising enabled by new technologies. Yet the same technologies also enable the spread of conspiracy theories and the creation of an environment of polarization and mistrust. If truth and fact can travel more widely and quickly than ever, so can lies and disinformation. Donald Trump was both the product of these trends and a powerful accelerant.

In rallying extremists and white supremacists, Trump also brought home the enduring power of racism in American politics—using a bullhorn, as many noted, after years in which other politicians on the right used dog whistles. It was a very old story, alas. Many of the anti-majoritarian features and habits of American politics, Jamelle Bouie noted in the *New York Times*, are part of a racist inheritance "clearly downstream of a style of extreme political combat that came to fruition in the defense of human bondage."[5]

We offer this brief account of the many sources of our democracy's distemper to make clear that we do not see universal civic duty voting as the one and only step that must be taken to push back against our system's anti-majoritarian tendencies. We would urge many others as well, including the election of the president by popular vote, and statehood for the District of Columbia and Puerto Rico—a step to right the underrepresentation of minority communities in the Senate. We support an end to gerrymandering, the establishment of a matching fund system for small political donors to challenge the power of big money, and a host of other reforms we have already described.

Yet if we see grave challenges to democratic values at the start of the third decade of the twenty-first century, we also see many signs of a democratic renewal. We cheer the mobilization of new forces on behalf of democratic change, an invigorated movement against racism, popular demands for an active and competent government in the wake of the pandemic, and a new appreciation for democracy itself. The very threats democracy faced during the Trump years and the challenges it continues to confront both at home and around the world have reminded us of how precious liberty and self-government are—and how urgent it is to nurture them. This is indeed a time to think and act anew, to experiment boldly and persistently.

The widespread desire for a stronger democracy is why we believe universal civic duty voting has an unprecedented fighting chance. Involving everyone in our system of government will create a voting population truly representative of all Americans. It will also expand confidence in our democratic system. Civic duty voting is a necessary step toward completing our nation's long struggle for inclusion. It is the essential antidote to anti-majoritarianism—the reform that could undergird other reforms. It would tear down barriers and lift up our civic obligations. It would bring us much closer to 100% democracy.

Authors' Note and Acknowledgments

100% Democracy builds on the strong platform constructed by the Working Group on Universal Voting, which the authors organized under the auspices of the Brookings Institution and the Ash Center for Democratic Governance and Innovation at Harvard's Kennedy School. We are deeply appreciative of the two institutions' unwavering support for this work, especially that of Darrell West at Brookings and Archon Fung at the Ash Center.

The book draws from and substantially expands upon the working group's report, "Lift Every Voice: The Urgency of Universal Civic Duty Voting." We honor the members of the working group by listing them in Appendix B. It is a small way to pay a large debt. Our discussions over eighteen months helped clarify the issues at stake and reinforced our excitement about what universal civic duty voting could achieve. Their ideas helped shape this book.

We feel a particular debt to the scholars and lawyers who drafted the legal analysis of the proposal's constitutionality: Allegra Chapman, Joshua Douglas, Cecily Hines, and Brenda Wright. Their work appears in these pages in Chapter Five largely as they wrote it. We also owe a deep debt to Cornell William Brooks, Amber Herrle, and Janai Nelson, whose contributions were indispensable. Quotations in the book from Brooks and Nelson come from events organized around the original report or from conversations with the authors; their keen eye for history and for the implications of universal voting for Black Americans and other communities of color was essential. Herrle was central to the entire project, organizing its meetings and playing a key role in drafting the original report. Shane Singh, even though he was working on a book of his own on this topic, was exceptionally generous in helping us draft the chapter on lessons from abroad. That chapter owes a great deal to the labors of Singh and Herrle. And Megan Bell was essential in helping us transform the efforts of the working group into this volume.

Dionne offers special appreciation to his Brookings Institution colleague William Galston, with whom he co-authored a 2015 Brookings paper in support of universal voting. That paper was a spark for the work that went into this book and influenced it in important ways.

The working group is continuing, helping to move universal civic duty voting into the public debate. But while these independent-minded citizens join in supporting the concept of universal civic duty voting, they are not accountable for what we have written here. This book reflects our views, choices, emphases, and conclusions.

Nelson, associate director-counsel of the NAACP Legal Defense and Educational Fund, noted that universal voting would not only "broaden the opportunity for every eligible voter to participate in our democracy" but also, in the process, "engage more voters in the conversation and in the democratic experience, bringing historically disenfranchised voters into our democracy. This would enable transformative change in a way that we've never seen it before."

  We agree.

———

You would not be reading this book were it not for Diane Wachtell, our brilliant and visionary editor at The New Press. Diane reached out to us while we were engaged with the Working Group and said she had long wanted a book on the topic of (to use our phrase) universal civic duty voting. We embraced the opportunity. She not only returned our enthusiasm but also did what great editors do. She offered invaluable suggestions on how to organize the book, provided superb line edits, asked excellent questions about what we were trying to say, and gave us thoughtful ideas about how we might say it. She has been a champion and a warm friend throughout.

  The New Press is blessed with extraordinary people at all levels. We are deeply grateful that Ellen Adler, the publisher, welcomed this book with great enthusiasm from the start. Rachel Vega-DeCesario made everything efficient—from the brilliant design of the cover and interior of the book to the editing—and did so with great warmth and cheer. Speaking of design, thanks to Ben Denzer for a cover we liked instantly, and to Bookbright Media for the interior design and typesetting. Susan Warga was a superb copy editor and Emily Albarillo was a wonderful and responsive production editor. And this book would not be in your hands (or on your screen) were it not for the exceptional care, energy, commitment, flexibility, and wisdom throughout of senior managing editor Maury Botton. He is, if we may put it this way, a 100% great managing editor who always has the reader in mind.

We already thanked Megan Bell of the Brookings Institution for her work on the original report on civic duty voting. Her extraordinary, tireless, careful, and thoughtful work was even more critical to the production of this volume. Thanks also to Brookings interns Johanna Bandler, Sonali Deliwala, and Grayson Peters for research, fact-checking and great help on our extensive footnotes.

And special thanks to Heather McGhee for her exceptional leadership and her eloquence in standing up for a just multiracial America. We are deeply honored and grateful that she graced this book with her Foreword.

From Miles Rapoport: I have always considered myself an organizer, and part of a progressive movement for justice and democracy. I have had extraordinary partners and friends all along the way; this book is in large part a result of all the work we have done together and all that I have learned from them. My colleagues in Mass Fair Share, the Connecticut Citizen Action Group, Citizen Action, DemocracyWorks, Dēmos, Common Cause, the Ash Center, and so many friends and colleagues in progressive politics in Connecticut are all in different ways important contributors to this book.

I want to deeply thank my family, who have supported all the work I have done for many years: my wife and forty-five-year partner in politics and the journey of life, Sam Luciano; my sons Jeff and Ross; and my wonderful grandchildren Max, Gemma, and Gianna.

From E.J. Dionne: I have been blessed with many dear friends too numerous to name here who have instructed me about politics, democracy, and civic life. And I am forever grateful to have been able to work at extraordinary institutions full of inspiring people. Thanks to my colleagues at the Brookings Institution; the Washington Post; Georgetown University, particularly the McCourt School of Public Policy; and Harvard University, particularly the Divinity School, the Kennedy School of Government, and the Committee on Degrees in Social Studies.

Nothing I say here will be an adequate expression of my love for Mary Boyle and our children, James, Julia, and Margot. I can only say how grateful I am for the wisdom they have shared with me every day and for the deep commitment all of them have to the joys and responsibilities of democratic life.

Lastly, we want to thank each other. Our partnership in defense of a vision of how democracy can and should work has been a delight to each of us. We also hope it will help advance more inclusive forms of civic and political life in our nation.

Appendix A

A Model Universal Civic Duty Voting Bill

In January 2021, State Senator Will Haskell introduced a universal civic duty voting bill in the Connecticut state legislature. This is the text of his bill.

Proposed S.B. No. 180
Session Year 2021

AN ACT CONCERNING UNIVERSAL CIVIC DUTY VOTING.

Statement of Purpose: To make several changes designed to institute universal civic duty voting.

Introduced by:

Sen. Will Haskell, 26th Dist.

AN ACT CONCERNING UNIVERSAL CIVIC DUTY VOTING. Be it enacted by the Senate and House of Representatives in General Assembly convened: That title 9 of the general statutes be amended to provide that (1) at the 2024 state election and each state election thereafter, all

qualified electors shall either cast a ballot or provide a valid reason for not casting a ballot, (2)
following the 2024 state election and each state
election thereafter, (A) the Secretary of the State
shall mail to all qualified electors who did not
cast a ballot at the most recent state election a
form inquiring as to why such elector did not
cast a ballot, which form shall advise that valid
reasons for not casting a ballot include travel, illness, conscientious objection or such other reason as the Secretary may prescribe, and (B) failure to respond to such form with a valid reason
shall result in a fine of twenty dollars paid to the
Office of the Secretary of the State, which fine
shall (i) not be increased through penalty fees or
accrued interest, (ii) not be the basis for criminal
enforcement or denial of government services or
benefits, and (iii) be directed to the State Elections Enforcement Commission for deposit in the
Citizens' Election Fund, except that an elector
may perform two hours of community service
for a Connecticut-based nonprofit organization
if such elector is unable to pay such fine, (3) one
month prior to the 2024 state election, the Secretary of the State shall mail to all qualified elec-

tors a notice that (A) explains the changes that
will take effect beginning at the 2024 state election, as described herein, and (B) includes a statement that each qualified elector will be required
to either cast a ballot, with the option to leave
such ballot blank, or provide a valid reason for
not casting a ballot, (4) at the 2022 state election
and each state election thereafter, each ballot
shall include in sufficiently large type a statement
advising electors that they may leave any portion
or the entirety of such ballot blank, and (5) not
later than January 1, 2025, the Secretary of the
State shall report on the implementation of such
changes, as described herein, at the 2024 state
election to the joint standing committee of the
General Assembly having cognizance of matters
relating to elections.

Appendix B

The Working Group on
Universal Voting

By way of expressing our gratitude, we list here the members of the working group that we described in our authors' note. Its members are not responsible for the contents of this book, but they taught us a great deal, and they inspired us. (Their organizations are listed for identification purposes only.)

Michelle Bishop, National Disability Rights Network
Cornell William Brooks, Harvard Kennedy School
Nick Chedli Carter, Resilient Democracy Fund
Allegra Chapman, Chapman Consulting and Common Cause
Cheryl Clyburn Crawford, Mass VOTE
Joshua A. Douglas, University of Kentucky Rosenberg College of Law
Anthony Fowler, The University of Chicago
Archon Fung, The Ash Center for Democratic Governance and Innovation, Harvard Kennedy School
William A. Galston, The Brookings Institution
Joseph Goldman, The Democracy Fund

Amber Herrle, The Brookings Institution

Cecily Hines, The Ash Center for Democratic Governance and Innovation, Harvard Kennedy School

María Teresa Kumar, Voto Latino

Carolyn J. Lukensmeyer, National Institute for Civil Discourse

Thomas E. Mann, The Brookings Institution

Terry Ao Minnis, Asian Americans Advancing Justice I AAJC

Janai Nelson, NAACP Legal Defense and Educational Fund

Nick Nyhart, Nyhart Consulting

Norman J. Ornstein, American Enterprise Institute

Andre M. Perry, The Brookings Institution

Whitney Quesenbery, Center for Civic Design

Ian Simmons, Blue Haven Initiative

Shane P. Singh, University of Georgia

Tova Wang, The Ash Center for Democratic Governance and Innovation, Harvard Kennedy School

Dorian Warren, Community Change

Brenda Wright, Dēmos

Notes

Introduction

1. Marc E. Elias (@marceelias), "No one should have to bring a lawn chair and a lunchbox to vote. Long lines are voter suppression in action," Twitter, June 18, 2020, 10:01 a.m., https://twitter.com/marceelias/status/1273616769706602496?s=21.

2. The voting rights advocate and Du Bois are quoted in Eric Foner, *The Second Founding: How the Civil War and Reconstruction Remade the Constitution* (New York: Norton, 2019), 94–95.

3. Ronald Brownstein, "False Fraud Claims Fanned Capitol Riot. Now They're Fueling GOP Efforts to Restrict Voting," CNN Politics, January 12, 2021.

4. Joshua B. Douglas, "Republicans aren't just making it harder to vote. They're going after election officials, too," *The Washington Post*, May 9, 2021.

5. Jamelle Bouie, "'Stop the Steal Didn't Start with Trump," *The New York Times*, January 15, 2021.

6. Rev. Martin Luther King Jr., "I Have a Dream," March on Washington (1963), available at https://www.archives.gov/files/press/exhibits/dream-speech.pdf.

7. United States Elections Project, "National General Election VEP Turnout Rates, 1789–Present," http://www.electproject.org/national-1789-present.

8. We are grateful to PRRI for running a specific analysis on the 2016 American Values Survey for us. The 2016 American Values Survey is available here: https://www.prri.org/wp-content/uploads/2016/10/PRRI-2016-American-Values-Survey.pdf.

9. Knight Foundation, "The 100 Million Project: The Untold Story of American Non-Voters," February 2020, https://knightfoundation.org/wp-content/uploads/2020/02/The-100-Million-Project_KF_Report_2020.pdf.

10. See Foner, *The Second Founding*.

11. Lisa Hill, "Compulsory Voting Defended," in Jason Brennan and Lisa Hill, *Compulsory Voting: For and Against* (New York: Cambridge University Press, 2014), 197.

12. King quoted in Barbara Arnwine and John Nichols, "Martin Luther King's Call to 'Give Us the Ballot' Is as Relevant Today as It Was in 1957," *The Nation*, January 15, 2018.

13. This section draws on William A. Galston and E.J. Dionne Jr., "The Case for Universal Voting: Why Making Voting a Duty Would Enhance Our Elections and Improve Our Government," Brookings Institution Center for Effective Public Management, September 2015.

14. Joshua Kleinfeld and Rachel Kleinfeld, "How to Hold Elections During a Pandemic," *National Review*, April 7, 2020.

15. Joshua A. Douglas, *Vote for Us: How to Take Back Our Elections and Change the Future of Voting* (Amhert, NY: Prometheus Books), 209.

Chapter One: What We Learned in 2020

1. Alison Dirr, "9:04 p.m. An hour after polls closed, a long line at Riverside voting site," *Milwaukee Journal Sentinel,* April 7, 2020.

2. Republican Nat'l Comm. v. Democratic Nat'l Comm., 140 S. Ct. 1205, 1208 (2020) (Ginsburg, J., dissenting).

3. Aaron Blake, "Trump just comes out and says it: The GOP is hurt when it's easier to vote," *The Washington Post*, March 30, 2020.

4. Blake, "Trump just comes out and says it: The GOP is hurt when it's easier to vote.".

5. Philip Bump, "Trump, who has lied about voting for years, disparages voting by mail for self-serving reasons," *The Washington Post,* April 8, 2020.

6. Scott Bauer, "Trump loses Wisconsin case while arguing another one," *The Associated Press*, December 12, 2020.

7. Jonathan Martin, Maggie Haberman, and Nicholas Fandos, "McConnell Privately Backs Impeachment as House Moves to Charge Trump," *The New York Times,* January 12, 2021.

8. George Pillsbury, Caroline Mak, and Brian Miller, "America Goes to the Polls 2020," Nonprofit VOTE and the U.S. Elections Project, March 2021, https://www.nonprofitvote.org/documents /2021/03/america-goes-polls-2020.pdf/: 14.

Chapter Two: The Road to 2020

1. Ted Enamorado, "Georgia's 'Exact Match' Law Could Potentially Harm Many Eligible Voters," *The Washington Post,* October 20, 2018.

2. Christopher Ingraham, "This anti-voter-fraud program gets it wrong over 99 percent of the time. The GOP wants to take it nationwide," *The Washington Post*, July 20, 2017.

3. E.J. Dionne Jr., "Republicans Are Scared of Stacey Abrams. They Should Be," *The Washington Post*, October 24, 2018.

4. Cheryl L. Johnson, "Statistics of the Congressional Election of November 6, 2018," Office of the Clerk, U.S. House of Representatives, http://clerk.house.gov/member_info/electionInfo/2018 /statistics2018.pdf. For the 2014 election, see Karen Haas, "Statistics of the Congressional Election of November 4, 2014," Office of the Clerk, U.S. House of Representatives, https://history.house.gov /Institution/Election-Statistics/.

5. Jens Manuel Krogstad, Luis Noe-Bustamante, and Antonio Flores, "Historic Highs in 2018 Voter Turnout Extended Across Racial and Ethnic Groups," Pew Research Center, May 1, 2019, https://www.pewresearch.org/fact-tank/2019/05/01/historic-highs -in-2018-voter-turnout-extended-across-racial-and-ethnic-groups/.

6. George Pillsbury and Caroline Mak, "America Goes to the Polls 2018," Nonprofit VOTE and the U.S. Elections Project, March 2019, https://www.nonprofitvote.org/documents/2019/03 /america-goes-polls-2018.pdf/.

7. Jordan Misra, "Voter Turnout Rates Among All Voting

Age and Major Racial and Ethnic Groups Were Higher Than in 2014," U.S. Census Bureau, April 23, 2019, https://www.census .gov/library/stories/2019/04/behind-2018-united-states-midterm -election-turnout.html.

8. Eleanor Watson, "New Data Indicates a Massive Surge in Hispanic Voter Turnout," CBS News, July 10, 2019.

Chapter Three: The Paradox of a Crisis

1. Lara Putnam and Theda Skocpol, "Middle America Reboots Democracy," *Democracy Journal*, February 20, 2018.

2. "Estimated Costs of Covid-19 Resiliency Measures," Brennan Center for Justice, April 18, 2020, https://www.brennancenter .org/our-work/research-reports/estimated-costs-covid-19-election -resiliency-measures.

3. E.J. Dionne Jr., "Saving Democracy Requires Voting Early— and Counting Fast," *The Washington Post*, September 16, 2020.

4. Joe Biden, "Remarks by President Biden on Protecting the Sacred, Constitutional Right to Vote," July 13, 2021, https://www.whitehouse.gov/briefing-room/speeches-remarks /2021/07/13/remarks-by-president-biden-on-protecting-the-sacred -constitutional-right-to-vote.

5. "Voting Laws Roundup: October 2021," Brennan Center for Justice, October 4, 2021. https://www.brennancenter.org/our -work/research-reports/voting-laws-roundup-october-2021.

Chapter Four: Democracy Sausages, Required Voting, and High Turnout

1. Tacey Rychter, "How Compulsory Voting Works: Australians Explain," *The New York Times*, October 22, 2018.

2. All quotations from Kim Beazley are from an interview conducted over Zoom by E.J. Dionne with Beazley from the governor's office in Perth, Western Australia, on December 21, 2020.

3. Elizabeth Addonizio, Donald P. Green, and James M. Glaser,

"Putting the Party Back into Politics: An Experiment Testing Whether Election Day Festivals Increase Voter Turnout," *PS: Political Science and Politics* 40, no. 4 (2007): 721–27.

4. Ralph Nader, "Now More than Ever, Americans Should Be Required to Vote," *Playboy*, March 2, 2020, https://www.playboy .com/read/ralph-nader-opinion-compulsory-voting.

5. "O'Toole muses to virtual crowd about mandat-ory voting, look-ing to Australia," CTVNews (April 27, 2021). https://www.ctvnews.ca /politics/o-toole-muses-to-virtual-crowd-about-mandatory-voting -looking-to-australia-1.5404282.

6. Jill Lepore, "Rock, Paper, Scissors: How We Used to Vote," *The New Yorker*, October 6, 2008.

7. Eldon Cobb Evans, *A History of the Australian Ballot System in the United States* (Chicago: University of Chicago Press, 1917), 20–27; Lepore, "Rock, Paper, Scissors."

8. John Hirst, "The Distinctiveness of Australian Democracy," *Papers on Parliament* 42 (December 2004).

9. Hirst, "The Distinctiveness of Australian Democracy."

10. This section draws on William A. Galston and E.J. Dionne Jr., "The Case for Universal Voting: Why Making Voting a Duty Would Enhance Our Elections and Improve Our Government," Brookings Institution Center for Effective Public Management, September 2015.

11. Anthony Fowler, "Electoral and Policy Consequences of Voter Turnout: Evidence from Compulsory Voting in Australia," *Quarterly Journal of Political Science* 8 (2013): 159–82, quote on 180.

12. For enrollment figures, see Australian Electoral Commission, "Enrollment Statistics," December 31, 2020, https://www.aec.gov .au/enrolling_to_vote/enrolment_stats/.

13. Vote-by-mail ballots that were cast before 6:00 p.m. on election day and are received within thirteen days of polls closing are counted.

14. Damon Muller, "Trends in Early Voting in Federal Elections," *FlagPost* (blog), Parliament of Australia,

August 5, 2019, https://www.aph.gov.au/About_Parliament
/Parliamentary_Departments/Parliamentary_Library/FlagPost
/2019/May/Trends_in_early_voting_in_federal_elections.

15. We note that alternative voting rates vary greatly by state, geography, and resource disparities. For more information, see the table "Percentage of Voters That Used Alternative Methods of Voting by State: Midterm Elections 2014 and 2018," in Jordan Misra, "Voter Turnout Rates Among All Voting Age and Major Racial and Ethnic Groups Were Higher than in 2014," U.S. Census Bureau, April 23, 2019, https://www.census.gov/library/stories
/2019/04/behind-2018-united-states-midterm-election-turnout
.html.

16. Australian Electoral Commission, "Practise Voting," last updated March 25, 2019, https://aec.gov.au/Voting/How_to_vote
/practice/.

17. Australian Electoral Commission, "2018–2019 Annual Report," September 2019.

18. Australian Electoral Commission, "AEC Report to JSCEM on Non-voting and Multiple Voting at 2007 Federal Election," April 2009.

19. Australian Electoral Commission, "Enrolment Statistics"; Australian Electoral Commission, "Indigenous Enrolment Rate," September 4, 2020, https://www.aec.gov.au/Enrolling_to_vote
/Enrolment_stats/performance/indigenous-enrolment-rate.htm.

20. Kathy Gilsinan, "Why Is It Illegal to Not Vote in Most of Latin America?," *The Atlantic*, October 26, 2014.

21. Sarah Birch, *Full Participation: A Comparative Study of Compulsory Voting* (New York: United Nations University Press, 2009); Jean Stengers, "Histoire de la legislation électorale en Belgique," *Revue belge de philologie et d'histoire* 82, nos. 1–2 (2004): 247–70.

22. Birch, *Full Participation*.

23. Missouri Supreme Court, *Reports of Cases Determined by the Supreme Court of the State of Missouri*, vol. 136 (1897), 475.

24. Henry J. Abraham, "What Cure for Voter Apathy?," *National*

Civic Review 41, no. 7 (1952): 346–57; Simon Jackman, "Compulsory Voting," in *International Encyclopedia of the Social and Behavioral Sciences*, ed. Neil J. Smelser and Paul B. Baltes (Oxford: Elsevier, 2001): 16314–18; Massachusetts Constitution, article LXI.

25. James D. Barnett, "Compulsory Voting in Oregon," *American Political Science Review* 15, no. 2 (1921): 265–66.

26. John M. Carey and Yusaku Horiuchi, "Compulsory Voting and Income Inequality," paper prepared for the Annual Workshop on the Frontiers of Statistical Analysis and Formal Theory of Political Science, January 2, 2014, https://cpb-us-e1.wpmucdn.com/sites.dartmouth.edu/dist/2/109/files/2013/02/CH-Compulsory-Voting-Income-Inequality-010214.pdf.

27. Steven Bodzin, "Chile Drops Mandatory Vote—and a Few Incumbent Mayors," *The Christian Science Monitor*, October 29, 2012.

28. Shane P. Singh, *Beyond Turnout: How Compulsory Voting Shapes Citizens and Political Parties* (New York: Oxford University Press, 2021), manuscript excerpt made available to authors before publication.

29. On Norway travel vouchers and Bulgarian lottery, see John Duffy and Alexander Matros, "On the Use of Fines and Lottery Prizes to Increase Voter Turnout," *Economics Bulletin* 34, no. 2 (2014): 966–75.

30. Howard Blume, "Voter in L.A. School Board Race Wins $25,000 for Casting a Ballot," *Los Angeles Times*, July 17, 2015.

31. Blume, "Voter in L.A. School Board Race."

32. "Arizona Voter Reward, Proposition 200 (2006)," Ballotpedia, https://ballotpedia.org/Arizona_Voter_Reward,_Proposition_200_(2006)#cite_note-quotedisclaimer-2).

33. Birch, *Full Participation*; "Estos son los incentivos para votar este domingo," *El Nuevo Siglo* (Bogotá), March 2, 2021.

34. Jonathan S. Gould and Nicholas Stephanopoulos, "Pay People to Vote," *The Atlantic*, August 10, 2021.

35. Carolina A. Fornos, Timothy J. Power, and James C. Garand, "Explaining Voter Turnout in Latin America, 1980 to 2000," *Comparative Political Studies* 37, no. 8 (2004): 909–40; Costas Panagopoulos, "The Calculus of Voting in Compulsory Voting Systems," *Political Behavior* 30, no. 4 (2008): 455–67; Shane P. Singh, "How Compelling Is Compulsory Voting? A Multilevel Analysis of Turnout," *Political Behavior* 33, no. 1 (2011): 95–111.

36. Ruth Dassonneville, Marc Hooghe, and Peter Miller, "The Impact of Compulsory Voting on Inequality and the Quality of the Vote," *West European Politics* 40, no. 3 (2017): 621–44; Mitchell Hoffman, Gianmarco León, and María Lombardi, "Compulsory Voting, Turnout, and Government Spending: Evidence from Austria," *Journal of Public Economics* 145, no. 1 (2017): 103–15; Shane P. Singh, "Compulsory Voting and the Turnout Decision Calculus," *Political Studies* 63, no. 3 (2015): 548–68; Gabriel Cepaluni and F. Daniel Hidalgo, "Compulsory Voting Can Increase Political Inequality: Evidence from Brazil," *Political Analysis* 24, no. 2 (2016): 273–80.

37. Timothy J. Power and James C. Garand, "Determinants of Invalid Voting in Latin America," *Electoral Studies* 26, no. 2 (2007): 432–44; Shane P. Singh, "Politically Unengaged, Distrusting, and Disaffected Individuals Drive the Link Between Compulsory Voting and Invalid Balloting," *Political Science Research and Methods* 7, no. 1 (2019): 107–23; Fredrik Uggla, "Incompetence, Alienation, or Calculation? Explaining Levels of Invalid Ballots and Extra-Parliamentary Votes," *Comparative Political Studies* 41, no. 8 (2008): 1141–64.

38. Ange McCormack, "How 'Wasted' Informal Votes Could Have Determined the Election," Australian Broadcasting Company, July 4, 2016.

39. Singh, "Politically Unengaged."

40. Ruth Dassonneville, Fernando Feitosa, Marc Hooghe, Richard R. Lau, and Dieter Stiers, "Compulsory Voting Rules, Reluctant Voters, and Ideological Proximity Voting," *Political Behavior* 41,

no. 1 (2019): 209–30; Peter Selb and Romain Lachat, "The More, the Better? Counterfactual Evidence on the Effect of Compulsory Voting on the Consistency of Party Choice," *European Journal of Political Research* 48, no. 5 (2009): 573–97; Shane P. Singh, "Elections as Poorer Reflections of Preferences Under Compulsory Voting," *Electoral Studies* 44, no. 1 (2016): 56–65; Jeremy Ferwerda, "Electoral Consequences of Declining Participation: A Natural Experiment in Austria," *Electoral Studies* 35, no. 1 (2014): 242–52; Christian B. Jensen and Jae-Jae Spoon, "Compelled Without Direction: Compulsory Voting and Party System Spreading," *Electoral Studies* 30, no. 4 (2011): 700–711.

41. See, e.g., Michael M. Bechtel, Dominik Hangartner, and Lukas Schmid, "Does Compulsory Voting Increase Support for Leftist Policy?," *American Journal of Political Science* 60, no. 3 (2016): 752–67; Anthony Fowler, "Electoral and Policy Consequences of Voter Turnout: Evidence from Compulsory Voting in Australia," *Quarterly Journal of Political Science* 8, no. 2 (2013): 159–82; Hoffman, León, and Lombardi, "Compulsory Voting"; Peter Miller and Ruth Dassonneville, "High Turnout in the Low Countries: Partisan Effects of the Abolition of Compulsory Voting in the Netherlands," *Electoral Studies* 44, no. 1 (2016): 132–43.

42. On income inequality, see John M. Carey and Yusaku Horiuchi, "Compulsory Voting and Income Inequality: Evidence for Lijphart's Proposition from Venezuela," *Latin American Politics and Society* 59, no. 2 (2017): 122–44; Alberto Chong and Mauricio Olivera, "Does Compulsory Voting Help Equalize Incomes?," *Economics and Politics* 20, no. 3 (2008): 391–415. On attachment to political parties, see Russel J. Dalton and Steven Weldon, "Partisanship and Party System Institutionalization," *Party Politics* 13, no. 2 (2007): 179–96; Shane P. Singh and Judd Thornton, "Compulsory Voting and the Dynamics of Partisan Identification," *European Journal of Political Research* 52, no. 2 (2013): 188–211.

43. Shane P. Singh, "Compulsory Voting and Parties' Vote-Seeking Strategies," *American Journal of Political Science* 63, no. 1 (2019): 37–52.

Chapter Five: Establishing Justice, Securing the Blessings of Liberty

1. The First Amendment of the United States Constitution guarantees that "Congress shall make no law . . . abridging the freedom of speech." This protection applies at both federal and state levels, thanks to the Fourteenth Amendment's prohibition against the states depriving individuals of liberty without due process of law, and any First Amendment analysis of a mandatory voting program's constitutionality would apply whether Congress, a state legislature, or a local body enacted such a requirement.

2. *West Virginia State Board of Education v. Barnette*, 63 S.Ct. 1178, 1183, 319 U.S. 624, 633 (1943); second quote at 645 (Murphy, J., concurring). In this case, a Jehovah's Witness family filed suit against the local school district when their children were threatened with both reform school and delinquency, a punishable crime, after refusing to salute the flag and recite the pledge of allegiance. In a 6–3 decision, the Court declared the salute (plus pledge) "a form of utterance" (or expressive conduct), and held that the school's requiring students to either perform it or be expelled was a violation of their First and Fourteenth Amendment rights.

3. In *Wooley v. Maynard*, private citizens sued New Hampshire officials for requiring use of license tags with the "Live Free or Die" motto; the Supreme Court agreed that the underlying law amounted to a First Amendment violation given that it required individuals to "use their private property as a 'mobile billboard' for the State's ideological message." 97 S.Ct. 1428, 1435, 430 U.S. 705, 715 (1977). In *Pacific Gas & Electric Co. v. Public Utilities Commission*, the Supreme Court held that a state may not "require a privately owned utility company to include in its billing envelopes speech of a third party with which the utility disagree[d]."

4. See *Spence v. Washington*, 418 U.S. 405 (1974).

5. Sean Matsler, "Compulsory Voting in America," 76 *Southern California Law Review* 76, no. 4 (2003): 972. As a counter-

argument, some may claim the government's compelling election "attendance"—even just for purposes of signing in—is itself a First Amendment violation insofar as showing up, with nothing more, amounts to a form of speech demonstrating support for the democratic process and for voting more specifically. That "anarchist" argument, though, likely fails for the same reason claims that filing and paying taxes, showing up for jury duty, and registering for signing up for Selective Service all violate the First Amendment likely fail: all implicate expression, but they are nevertheless forms of conduct the government may regulate.

Alternatively, a "universal voting" model in which individuals would be compelled to select a candidate (rather than being able to reject all candidates) would almost certainly be considered a free-speech violation. As Matsler notes, "Voting for a candidate—not selection of the 'none of the above' option . . . is similar to other nonverbal acts, such as wearing of a black armband to signify disagreement with the Vietnam War, that have received First Amendment protection from the Supreme Court in the past." Further, "Requiring someone to vote for a particular cause or candidate would clearly violate the First Amendment, but requiring someone to vote for the candidate of his or her choosing is viewpoint neutral." Many would debate the constitutionality of the government requiring a citizen to vote for a candidate, even if the citizen had the option of choosing which one. A civic duty voting requirement, as we propose it, wouldn't compel any vote at all, and thus wouldn't compel speech. The fact that this conduct may implicate the use of language is not dispositive; instead, the question becomes whether *this very engagement* with the voting system could be considered expressive conduct subject to First Amendment protections.

6. See, e.g., *United States v. Lee*, 455 U.S. 252, 260 (1982) (rejecting argument that a requirement to pay taxes violates the First Amendment rights of those who have religious or moral objections); *Wayte v. United States*, 470 U.S. 598 (1985) (rejecting First Amendment challenge to prosecution for not registering for the Selective Service).

7. Note that incidental implications on speech were a deciding factor for the Court in rejecting a First Amendment challenge in which a group of law schools challenged the power of the federal government to condition university funding on their granting equal access to the military at campus recruitment events, as compared to other recruiters. See *Rumsfeld v. Forum for Academic and Institutional Rights, Inc.*, 126 S.Ct. 1297, 1310, 547 U.S. 47, 59 (2006) (citing *Hurley v. Irish-American Gay, Lesbian and Bisexual Group of Boston, Inc.*, 515 U.S. 557, 566, 115 S.Ct. 2338, 132 L.Ed.2d 487 [1995] [emphasis added]). The plaintiff schools claimed that their decision to block access to military recruiters on campus was expressive of their disagreement with the "don't ask, don't tell" policy. The Supreme Court, however, held that, in addition to the established power of the government to condition funds for any action that it could otherwise regulate directly (see, e.g., *United States v. American Library Assn., Inc.*, 539 U.S. 194, 210, 123 S.Ct. 2297, 156 L.Ed.2d 221), the statute itself did not implicate protections against compelled speech because it "affect[ed] what law schools must *do*—afford equal access to military recruiters—not what they may or may not *say*." It "neither limit[ed] what law schools may say nor require[d] them to say anything." Beyond the kinds of literal "speech" necessary to meet the minimum requirement of granting equal access (e.g., sending emails between staff, posting the list of employers that will be attending recruitment events on their website, etc.), the schools were free to "express whatever views they may have on the military's congressionally mandated employment policy," from ignoring them to publishing their severest disapproval. There was nothing about a recruitment event, according to the Court, that would affect the ability of the university to "choose the content of [their] own message," since they "remained free to disassociate [themselves] from those views [with which they disagreed] and . . . [were] 'not . . . being compelled to affirm [a] belief in any governmentally prescribed position or view.'" *Rumsfeld v. Forum for Academic and Institutional Rights, Inc.*, 126 S.Ct. 1297, 1307, 1309, 1310, 547 U.S. 47, 60 (2006) (emphasis in original), citing *Pruneyard* at 88, 100 S.Ct. 2035.

8. There has been continuing discussion about whether the government should also compel women to register for the Selective Service. See Selective Service System, "Why Aren't Women Required to Register?", https://www.sss.gov/register/women/.

9. *United States v. O'Brien*, 88 S.Ct. 1673, 1678, 391 U.S. 367, 376 (1968).

10. *United States v. O'Brien*, 88 S.Ct. 1673, 1679, 391 U.S. 367, 377 (1968).

11. "The Case for Compulsory Voting in America," *Harvard Law Review* 121, no. 2 (2007): 602.

12. As was established by the Court in 1968: a government regulation is sufficiently justified if it is within the constitutional power of the Government [caps in the original], if it furthers an important or substantial governmental interest, if the governmental interest is unrelated to the suppression of free expression, and if the incidental restriction on alleged First Amendment freedoms is no greater than is essential to the furtherance of that interest. See *United States v. O'Brien*, 88 S.Ct. 1673, 1679, 391 U.S. 367, 377 (1968).

13. *Burdick v. Takushi*, 504 U.S. 428, 434 (1992).

14. *Burdick v. Takushi*, 112 S.Ct. 2059, 2063–64, 504 U.S. 428, 434 (1992), citing *Anderson v. Celebrezze*, 103 S.Ct. 1564, 1569–70, 460 U.S. 780, 788 (1983). See also Richard L. Hasen, "Voting Without Law?," *University of Pennsylvania Law Review* 144 (1996): 2135. The content-neutral First Amendment restriction in *Burdick* was Hawaii's prohibition on write-in voting. And though it did affect the manner of voting—burdening voters' "limited interest in waiting until the eleventh hour to choose [their] preferred candidate"—that statute was upheld when weighed against the state's constitutionally adequate ballot access statutes and its important government interest in avoiding factionalism and "party raiding" (Hasen, "Voting Without Law," 1966). The Court, moreover, found that restrictions placed on voters in Hawaii were minimal because the state provided numerous ways for candidates to get their names on the primary ballot before the twenty-one-day cutoff date.

15. See Joshua A. Douglas, "Undue Deference to States in the 2020 Election Litigation," 2021, https://papers.ssrn.com/sol3 /papers.cfm?abstract_id=3720065.

16. Armand Derfner and J. Gerald Hebert, "Voting Is Speech," *Yale Law & Policy Review* 34, no. 2 (2016): 471–92. See also Allegra Chapman, "Is the Supreme Court at Odds with Itself When It Comes to Democracy?," *Election Law Journal* 16, no. 1 (2017): 142–52.

17. Derfner and Hebert, "Voting Is Speech," 471.

18. Derfner and Hebert, "Voting Is Speech," 485, 486, quoting *Wesbury, Sims, Anderson,* and others.

19. Janai S. Nelson, "The First Amendment, Equal Protection, and Felon Disenfranchisement: A New Viewpoint," *Florida Law Review* 65 (2013): 111.

20. "The Case for Compulsory Voting in America," quoting *Duren v. Missouri*, 439 U.S. 357, 364–66 (1979) (in which the Court holds the state may compel jury service "because of the importance of having a criminal jury [being one] that represents a fair cross-section of the community").

21. *See United States v. Sloane*, 411 F.3d 643, 648 (6th Cir. 2005) (establishing that § 10307 applies to both federal and mixed elections but "would not apply to 'a *purely* local election, say for mayor, or for representative in a legislature, for sheriff, or for any other local office'" [quoting *United States v. Cianciulli*, 482 F.Supp. 585, 616 (quoting 111 Cong. Rec. 8424 [1965])]); *United States v. Bowman*, 636 F.2d 1003, 1011 (5th Cir. 1981) ("Congress may regulate any activity which exposes the federal aspects of the election to the possibility of corruption, whether or not the actual corruption takes place and whether or not the persons participating in such activity had a specific intent to expose the federal election to such corruption or possibility of corruption"); *United States v. McCranie*, 169 F.3d 723, 727 (11th Cir. 1999) ("Again, whether the federal candidate is opposed or unopposed is of little consequence because the integrity of a mixed federal-state election is marred by fraudulent

voting activities, even if these activities are only directed toward the state elections" (citing *United States v. Cole*, 41 F.3d 303 [7th Cir. 1994]). See also *United States v. Garcia*, 719 F.2d 99, 102 (5th Cir. 1999) (holding that the Constitution's necessary-and-proper clause and Article I grant Congress the authority to regulate mixed federal and state elections).

22. See, e.g., *United States v. Bowman*, 636 F.2d 1003 (5th Cir. 1981); *United States v. Garcia*, 719 F.2d 99 (5th Cir. 1983).

23. *Dansereau v. Ulmer*, 903 P.2d 555 (Alaska 1995); *Naron v. Prestage*, 469 So. 2d 83 (Mississippi 1985).

24. *Dansereau v. Ulmer*, 903 P.2d at 561. See Cal. Elec. Code § 18521 (stating that one may not offer compensation in exchange for "voting for any particular person"); Wash. Rev. Code Ann. § 29.85.060 (prohibiting any person from "directly or indirectly offering a bribe, reward, or any thing of value to a voter in exchange for the voter's vote for or against any person or ballot measure, or authorizing any person to do so ").

25. Minn. Stat. Ann. § 211B.13 ("A person who willfully, directly or indirectly, advances, pays, gives, promises, or lends any money, food, liquor, clothing, entertainment, or other thing of monetary value, or who offers promises, or endeavors to obtain any money, position, appointment, employment, or other valuable consideration, to or for a person, in order to induce a voter to refrain from voting, or to vote in a particular way, at an election is guilty of a felony"); Neb. Rev. Stat. § 32-1536 ("Any person who accepts or receives any valuable thing as a consideration for his or her vote for any person to be voted for at an election shall be guilty of a Class II misdemeanor"); N.H. Rev. Stat. Ann. § 659:40 ("No person shall directly or indirectly bribe any person not to register to vote or any voter not to vote or to vote for or against any question submitted to voters or to vote for or against any ticket or candidate for office at any election"); N.M. Stat. § 1-20-11 ("Offering a bribe consists of willfully advancing, paying, or causing to be paid, or promising, directly or indirectly, any money or valuable consideration,

office or employment, to any person for the following purposes connected with or incidental to an election: . . . to induce such a person, if a voter, to vote or refrain from voting for or against any candidate, proposition, question, or constitutional amendment"); 25 Pa. Stat. Ann. § 3539 ("Any person who shall, directly or indirectly, give or promise or offer to give any gift or reward in money, goods, or other valuable thing to any person, with intent to induce him to vote or refrain from voting for any particular candidate or candidates or for or against any constitutional amendment or other question at a primary or election; or who shall, directly or indirectly, procure for or offer or promise to procure for such person any such gift or reward with the intent aforesaid; or, who with the intent to influence or intimidate such person to give his vote or to refrain from giving his vote for any particular candidate or candidates . . . shall be guilty of a felony"); S.C. Code. Ann. § 7-25-60(A) ("It is unlawful for a person at any election to: (1) procure, or offer or propose to procure, another, by the payment, delivery, or promise of money or other article of value, to vote for or against any particular candidate or measure; or (2) vote, offer, or propose to vote for or against any particular candidate or measure for the consideration of money or other article of value paid, delivered, or promised, vote or offer or propose to vote for or against any particular candidate or measure"); Wash. Rev. Code Ann. § 29A.84.620; W. Va. Code Ann. § 3-9-13 ("It is unlawful for any person to offer or to pay money or any other thing of value to any person as consideration for the vote of the offeree or payee, as the case may be, to be cast for or against any candidate or issue in any election held in the state. Any person who violates the provisions of this subsection shall be guilty of a felony"); Wyo. Stat. Ann. § 22-26-109 ("Offering bribe consists of willfully advancing, paying, offering to pay or causing to be paid, or promising, directly or indirectly, any money or other valuable thing to a person, for any of the following purposes: . . . To induce a person to vote or refrain from voting for or against a candidate or ballot proposition or to sign or not sign a petition").

26. Joshua A. Douglas, "The Right to Vote Under Local Law,"

George Washington Law Review 85 (2017): 1073.

27. *New State Ice Co. v. Liebmann*, 285 U.S. 262, 311 (1932) (Brandeis, J., dissenting).

28. Douglas, "The Right to Vote Under Local Law," 1073.

29. Mass. Const. art. Article LXI ("The general court shall have authority to provide for compulsory voting at elections, but the right of secret voting shall be preserved").

30. Ohio Const. art. V, § 1.

31. See, e.g., Kentucky Const. § 145 ("Every citizen of the United States of the age of eighteen years who has resided in the state one year, and in the county six months, and the precinct in which he offers to vote sixty days next preceding the election, shall be a voter in said precinct").

32. For citations to the specific state constitutional and statutory provisions in these states, see the chart in Douglas, "The Right to Vote Under Local Law," 1073.

33. Conn. Gen. Stat. § 7-192a; Me. Stat. tit. 30-A, § 2501; Me. Stat. tit. 21-A, § 111.

Chapter Six: The Need for Persuasion

1. Pew Research Center, "Elections in America: Concerns over Security, Divisions over Expanding Access to Voting," October 2018; Peter Moore, "Americans: Make Voting Easier, Not Mandatory," YouGov, March 30, 2015.

2. A good summary of these findings is Neil Howe, "Are Millennials Giving Up on Democracy?," *Forbes*, October 31, 2017.

Chapter Seven: Answering the Critics

1. President Barack Obama, "Remarks by the President to the City Club of Cleveland," Global Center for Health Innovation, Cleveland, OH, March 18, 2015, https://obamawhitehouse .archives.gov/the-press-office/2015/03/18/remarks-president-city -club-cleveland.

2. Jonah Goldberg, "Progressives Think That Mandatory Voting Would Help Them at the Polls," *National Review,* November 13, 2015.

3. Hans A. Von Spakovsky, "Compulsory Voting Is Unconstitutional," Heritage Foundation, April 1, 2015, http://www.heritage.org/ research/commentary/2015/4/compulsory-voting-is-unconstitutional.

4. Jason Brennan, "Mandatory Voting Would Be a Disaster," *The New York Times,* November 7, 2011.

5. David Harsanyi, "Mandatory Voting Is Authoritarian," *National Review,* November 25, 2020.

6. David Harsanyi, "We Must Weed Out Ignorant Americans from the Electorate," *The Washington Post,* May 20, 2016.

7. Harsanyi, "Mandatory Voting Is Authoritarian."

8. "Nevadans to Keep 'None of the Above' Ballot Option," CBS News, September 5, 2012.

9. Attila Ambrus, Ben Greiner, and Anita Zednik, "The Effect of a 'None of the Above' Ballot Paper Option on Voting Behavior and Election Outcomes," March 14, 2019. Economic Research Initiatives at Duke (ERID) Working Paper No. 277.

10. Bharti Jain, "Election Results: NOTA Garners 1.1% of Country's Total Vote Share," *Times of India,* May 17, 2014.

11. Gaus quoted in Jason Brennan and Lisa Hill, *Compulsory Voting: For and Against* (New York: Cambridge University Press, 2014): 10.

12. Thurgood Marshall writing in *Peters v. Kiff,* Warden Certiorari to the United States Court of Appeals for the Fifth Circuit, No. 71-5078, argued February 22, 1972, decided June 22, 1972, https://tile.loc.gov/storage-services/service/ll/usrep/usrep407/usrep407493/usrep407493.pdf.

13. Charles J. Ogletree Jr., foreword to Andrew Guthrie Ferguson, *Why Jury Duty Matters* (New York: NYU Press, 2013), xv–xvi.

14. Ogletree Jr., foreword to *Why Jury Duty Matters.*

15. Trevor Burrus, "Mandatory Voting Guarantees Ignorant Votes," Cato Institute, March 22, 2015.

16. Brennan and Hill, *Compulsory Voting: For and Against*, 44, 104, 83.

17. Brennan and Hill, *Compulsory Voting: For and Against*, 104–5.

18. V.O. Key, *The Responsible Electorate: Rationality and Presidential Voting, 1936 to 1960* (New York: Random House, 1966); Samuel Popkin, *The Reasoning Voter: Communication and Persuasion in Presidential Campaigns* (Chicago: University of Chicago Press, 1994), 7.

19. Demos and the watchdog group Common Cause have both written about this issue extensively.

Chapter Eight: Paving the Way for Universal Voting

1. "Online Voter Registration Overview," National Conference of State Legislatures, https://www.ncsl.org/research/elections-and -campaigns/electronic-or-online-voter-registration.aspx.

2. Anthony Fowler, "Does Voter Preregistration Increase Youth Participation?," *Election Law Journal: Rules, Politics, and Policy* 16 no. 4 (December 2017): 485–94; John Holbein and D. Sunshine Hillygus, "Making Young Voters: The Impact of Preregistration on Youth Turnout," Duke University, 2014, https://sites.duke.edu /hillygus/files/2014/07/Preregistration-10.22.14.pdf.

3. Wendy Underhill, "State Laws Governing Early Voting," National Conference of State Legislatures, October 22, 2020, https://www.ncsl.org/research/elections-and-campaigns/early-voting-in -state-elections.aspx.

4. Ethan Kaplan and Haishan Yuan, "Early Voting Laws, Voter Turnout, and Partisan Vote Composition: Evidence from Ohio," *American Economic Journal: Applied Economics* 12, no. 1 (2020): 32.

Chapter Nine: Getting from Here to There

1. Abraham Lincoln, "Second Annual Message to Congress," December 1, 1862, https://millercenter.org/the-presidency/presidential-speeches/december-1-1862-second-annual-message.

2. Australian Electoral Commission, "Electoral Backgrounder: Compulsory Voting," April 4, 2019, https://www.aec.gov.au/about_aec/publications/backgrounders/compulsory-voting.htm.

3. Matt Ford, "Samuel Alito's Boundless Contempt for Democracy," *The New Republic*, July 7, 2021.

Chapter Ten: From the Impossible to the Inevitable

1. *New State Ice Co. v. Liebmann*, 285 U.S. 262 (1932) (Brandeis, J., dissenting).

2. "The U.S. Needs a Democracy Overhaul. Here's What Biden's First Step Should Be," editorial, *The Washington Post*, January 2, 2021.

3. Nicholas Stephanopoulos, "A Feasible Roadmap to Compulsory Voting," *The Atlantic*, November 2, 2015.

Chapter Eleven: Securing Rights, Embracing Responsibilities

1. John Lewis, "Together, You Can Redeem the Soul of Our Nation," *The New York Times*, July 30, 2020.

2. Steven Levitsky and Daniel Ziblatt, "End Minority Rule," *The New York Times*, October 23, 2020.

3. Levitsky and Ziblatt, "End Minority Rule."

4. Tim Lau, "*Citizens United* Explained," Brennan Center for Justice (Dec. 12, 2019) https://www.brennancenter.org/our-work/research-reports/citizens-united-explained.

5. Jamelle Bouie, "America Holds onto an Undemocratic Assumption from Its Founding: That Some People Deserve More Power than Others," *The New York Times*, August 14, 2019.

About the Authors

E.J. Dionne Jr. is the author or co-author of eight books, including, most recently *Code Red: How Progressives and Moderates Can Unite to Save Our Country*. He is a senior fellow at the Brookings Institution, a syndicated columnist for the *Washington Post*, university professor at Georgetown University's McCourt School of Public Policy, and visiting professor at Harvard University. He lives in Bethesda, Maryland.

Miles Rapoport is the Senior Practice Fellow in American Democracy at the Ash Center for Democratic Governance and Innovation at the Harvard Kennedy School. He formerly served in the Connecticut state legislature and as secretary of the state. He also served as president of Dēmos and of Common Cause. He lives in West Hartford, Connecticut.

Publishing in the Public Interest

Thank you for reading this book published by The New Press. The New Press is a nonprofit, public interest publisher. New Press books and authors play a crucial role in sparking conversations about the key political and social issues of our day.

We hope you enjoyed this book and that you will stay in touch with The New Press. Here are a few ways to stay up to date with our books, events, and the issues we cover:

- Sign up at www.thenewpress.com/subscribe to receive updates on New Press authors and issues and to be notified about local events
- www.facebook.com/newpressbooks
- www.twitter.com/thenewpress
- www.instagram.com/thenewpress

Please consider buying New Press books for yourself; for friends and family; or to donate to schools, libraries, community centers, prison libraries, and other organizations involved with the issues our authors write about.

The New Press is a 501(c)(3) nonprofit organization. You can also support our work with a tax-deductible gift by visiting www.thenewpress.com/donate.